# PRAISE FOR *NONE*

"A bold, astute consideration of the c[...]
of living outside normative categorie[...]
  —*KIRKUS REVIEWS*

"Humane and heart-rending."
  —*THE GUARDIAN*

"A breath of fresh air. . . . There's no memoir like it."
  —*THE INDEPENDENT*

"What an astounding book! Thank you, Travis, for your honesty, open-ness, humor, and brilliance. I devoured this book."
  —ELLIOT PAGE, actor and author of *Pageboy: A Memoir*

"In *None of the Above* you will see how Travis Alabanza is one of the most talented storytellers of a generation. This work is a beautifully visceral insight into the ways Travis navigates the world around us. *None of the Above* is potent, engaging, hilarious, and beautiful, just like Travis."
  —JONATHAN VAN NESS, six-time Emmy-nominated host of
    *Queer Eye* and *New York Times* best-selling author of *Love That Story: Observations from a Gorgeously Queer Life* and *Over the Top: My Story*

"Travis Alabanza is a wise, hilarious, and sharp thinker—a writer who not only defies categorization but who makes categorization itself seem fussy and obsolete."
  —TORREY PETERS, author of *Detransition, Baby: A Novel*

"Travis Alabanza's words have power. An essential read for everyone."
  —SAM SMITH, singer and songwriter

"One of those times you are so profoundly grateful that someone has cracked open their head and allowed you to look around at the beautiful, sad, and remarkable parts that make them who they are. A gloriously specific, funny, and smart body of work."
  —CANDICE CARTY-WILLIAMS, author of *Queenie*

# None of the Above

## Reflections on Life Beyond the Binary

# Travis Alabanza

FOREWORD BY ALOK VAID-MENON

**THE FEMINIST PRESS**
AT THE CITY UNIVERSITY OF NEW YORK
NEW YORK CITY

Published in 2023 by the Feminist Press
at the City University of New York
The Graduate Center
365 Fifth Avenue, Suite 5406
New York, NY 10016

feministpress.org

First Feminist Press edition 2023

NEW YORK STATE OF OPPORTUNITY. | Council on the Arts   This book was made possible thanks to a grant from the New York State Council on the Arts with the support of Governor Kathy Hochul and the New York State Legislature.

First printing October 2023
Cover design by Canongate Books
Text design by Drew Stevens

Library of Congress Cataloging-in-Publication Data is available for this title.
ISBN 978-1-55861-034-7

PRINTED IN THE UNITED STATES OF AMERICA

*Like all my work, this book is firstly dedicated to my mum. Thank you for defying all the odds.*

*I would also like to dedicate this book to any trans person who is confused, questioning, or in the middle of change. This book is to honor that state as a place that still deserves dedication.*

*I love us.*

# Contents

Foreword: Trans Rights Are Human Rights      ix
by Alok Vaid-Menon

Prologue      1

*The Sea*      13

1. "So when did you know?"      15
2. "But I mean, *real* trans."      35
3. "Ladies, gentlemen, and those lucky enough      67
   to transcend gender."

*The Bearded Monster*      91

4. "This ain't a thing we do round here, son."      93
5. "So what do you want me to call it?"      119
6. "Children sacrificed to appease trans lobby."      149
7. "This is for us, baby, not for them."      177

Acknowledgments      205

FOREWORD

# Trans Rights Are Human Rights

## ALOK VAID-MENON

In a society where the slogan "trans rights are human rights" is received as more provocation than promise, perhaps it's a good idea to pull over for a few minutes and take inventory of our present moment. Thank goodness we have Travis Alabanza—funny, level-headed, and even-handed as ever. Routing, rousing us to go nowhere. Which is, it turns out, the most beautiful place. The place we have been looking for all along.

The times we live in are surreal. As trans and nonbinary people we are experiencing unprecedented visibility in media and popular culture, alongside a surfeit of anti-trans legislation seeking to recriminalize our ability to exist in public. We are both revered and reviled, interchangeably the crisis and the solution. We are sometimes evidence of the decadence of Western civilization, and other times the depravity of it. It's the epitome of the Dickensian refrain "It was the best of times, it was the worst of times," which means: it is a day like any other—absurd. Being alive is absurd. It's not that life imitates art; it's that life is art with all of its whimsy and woe. And memoir is where we go to remember that—how living is a creative act. Or rather: the creative act.

Memoir is many things. Among them: an elaborate game of show-and-tell. It's where we recall that basic premise that is so often ignored in the world off the page: everyone is their own universe. We can go through the same things and emerge different people. It's that radical alterity that brings us affinity with one another, draws us closer. We find ourselves in contradistinction—we need each other to figure out who we are.

Good memoirs, like edible gluten-free pasta, are hard to come by. But when they do, their familiar strangeness equips us with the tools to defamiliarize our own reality, reconsider and revise it anew. Travis's *None of the Above* is a good memoir because in sharing their story, they provoke us to reconsider our own. All of a sudden, our most stubborn and resolute truths are seen for what they are: stories we tell about ourselves that have become congealed through repeated retelling over time. And the thing about a story—like a gender—is that it can be rewritten.

The presumption behind the slogan "trans rights are human rights" is that trans and nonbinary people are considered human—a reality that the escalating rhythm of anti-trans hostility in the world calls into question. Here we are, a people reduced to a political belief, and—if we're lucky—a series of disjointed body parts, hormones, and chromosomes scattered in legislative policy proposals. In a world where our very existence is viewed as an opinion, what is being disputed is not our rights but our personhood.

Trans and nonbinary people know this well. We know that this has never been about the bathrooms or the pronouns. This has always been about our right to exist. We know that the closet is a cage where people put the parts of themselves that they don't want to see anymore, and they put us there, too, to keep their repression company. We know that the goal has always been about our disappearance: to make gender nonconformity obsolete, like analog television or a telegraph spitting beat poetry to a room of philistines. We know that we are fighting for our lives, for the fleshiness of them. To be more than a symbol or a metaphor, but to be human.

And that's precisely our problem. Because we spend so much time knowing how the world sees us, we forget to see ourselves. And Travis's work is a reminder of that crucial distinction: That it is possible, and necessary, to develop a point of view of ourselves as trans and nonbinary people outside of the cisgender gaze. And that even if we can't fully do so, it's still worth striving for. Travis steers us away from the judiciary, past the governments, back to ourselves. What are the stories we tell about ourselves, and why? And perhaps more importantly, what gets left behind on the cutting-room floor?

*None of the Above* lives there in the scraps: The uncouth and inconvenient parts of ourselves. The politically inexpedient parts. This is a treatise on trans ambivalence. In a society that requires trans people to be absolute in our self-conviction, or else be abandoned, Travis writes that they do not know if they would be trans in a world without gender norms, that their relationship with their gender is more fleeting than fixed. They write that they cannot isolate their sense of self from the world around them, which has taught them that certain things are masculine and certain things are feminine. That, for all their ideological commitment against the gender binary, they—and we—are still so deeply steeped in it. This is a treatise on imbrication. It posits that there is no outside, no pure space. That our selves and our stories are fundamentally communal. And therefore, so must be our deepest ruminations, the awkward and inopportune parts of ourselves that we don't often share with one another for fear of being misrecognized.

This is the genius of Travis's work. In departing from the conventional lore of trans memoir, Travis takes us to no-man's-land. (Though I suppose as nonbinary people, that's where we should have been all along!) They take our clandestine in-community group chats and project them onto the page like drive-through cinema. They take the internal monologues, the hesitations, the thoughts that precede speech, and splay them out like a fish. They take everything we don't write about in public because we're afraid it'll be used to undermine our legitimacy and erode the political gains we've made, and they put it on display in a permanent exhibition: a book. And they do this seemingly heretical act because they love us, not for who we should be, but for who we are. For our contradictions, inconsistencies, and hesitancies.

It's a courageous act, as most displays of love are, because in a world where we are attacked from the outside, the political program prescribes a unified front: within ourselves and our community. And in rejecting the simple stories— before and after, us and them, inside and outside—Travis bequeaths us a precious lesson: in our pursuit of humanity as trans and nonbinary people we are, perhaps, dehumanizing ourselves.

Yes, of course those who have taken a pledge of allegiance to the gender binary view all of us who strive beyond it as a security risk. Yes, of course those who believe that you can take the chaos of the world and churn it into two discrete categories sit front row at our disappearing act with raucous applause. But what of us: we who grow up with fear as a third lung that barks every time we open our mouths? we who first see ourselves in cartoon villains and the monsters in fairy tales we're told as kids? Do we see ourselves as human? And if we did, how would we act accordingly?

As trans and nonbinary people, because we must spend so much of our time and energy exonerating ourselves from the narratives cisgender people write about us, we've neglected the crucial task of exploring ourselves for ourselves. Much of what we put out into the world is recuperative: seeking to assuage other people's anxieties about us. But in this work, Travis suspends that imperative and invites us to tell our stories from a different place, unmediated by the cisgender gaze. To embark on the quiet, assiduous work of sketching a self-concept on our own terms—for which doubt is often the sharpest pencil.

Certainly, it's dehumanizing for trans people to be defined by the crude arithmetic of our anatomy. But isn't it also dehumanizing to define ourselves by our certainty? The pendulum, no matter how tedious and banal it finds its job, continues to swing both ways. In response to being told that we don't exist, we overcompensate with certainty that creates no room for our human doubt. In response to our fullness being abbreviated into a phase, we've responded with permanence: "I will feel this way forever." But forever, like a distant moon, is not a place habitable for human life. We humans tend to move, evolve, change. And that's okay.

Travis's call for ambivalence is not to sabotage the political grounds we have won nor to diminish the reality of deeply felt conviction. It comes from a gentler, more expansive place. Certainty has been weaponized as a form of tyranny against trans people. We shouldn't have to be perfect to be accepted; perfection is the myth—not us. Our access to healthcare shouldn't be contingent on certitude, because others should have no jurisdiction over what we do with our own bodies in the first place. Our access to fundamental rights shouldn't even be linked to our stories. Those rights should be undeniable and indisputable, because this is about our bodily autonomy, not about our ability to fit into social convention. Our dignity shouldn't only be afforded through recognition of our divinity or infallibility. It should be there without debate, regardless of how we narrate ourselves. Our cisgender brothers and sisters are not held to such extreme standards: they routinely access gender-affirming procedures and make vast, life-altering decisions without having to perform permanence.

Transmisogyny lives in the double standards. And in the face of all that, Travis's book makes standard that we get to be unruly. We get to be in perpetual transformation. We get to be human.

—Alok Vaid-Menon
New York City
March 2023

# Prologue

The only prologue I've written before this one was for the published script of my theater show, *Burgerz*.[1] I wrote it in haste, having forgotten the deadline was imminent. For opening night, I typed what I thought would count as a prologue in my iPhone notes, without any sense of a future reader in mind. In that prologue, I wrote how *Burgerz*—which was created after a burger was thrown at me in broad daylight—was about "making sense of this violence." I talked about how the show was trying to grapple with the reality of someone throwing a burger at me while they were yelling a transphobic slur. I said that the play aimed to figure out why and how it was happening; said the purpose of it was that, through understanding, we could stop this act from happening again. That by trying to understand why people throw burgers at trans people in public, in particular at me, I would feel better. Sure, there were other sentences in there as well. I included some words about being only twenty-two and having something published, about not quite believing that to immortalize something on paper you did not have to be white, or posh, or a man—all things I am not. Back then, I sensed a similar feeling to one that is trying to bubble up to the page now before

1. Travis Alabanza, *Burgerz* (London: Oberon Books, 2018).

1

I write this book: a questioning of worth. Not whether the words were valuable, but was I worthy of the words I aimed to write? Yet underneath those sentences alluding to my self-doubt, I could feel a simultaneous desire to show I had it all figured out, almost as an overcompensation. The only destination I was aiming for was that of understanding. I wanted to put an experience in a box, to tell myself and you why and how the specifics of transphobia toward nonbinary people exist, and then to move on. As if explaining the cause of the violence would decrease the pain. As if understanding was the end goal. As if understanding burgers being thrown at people was even possible.

I write this, my next prologue, three years on. Instead of writing it in five minutes before a show begins, the global pandemic has stopped all live shows and it feels like I am writing in the opposite of haste. I remain not entirely sure what a prologue's goal is, yet I carry on because it is what I assume I must do, a part of me wondering if it's just a thing posh people do to avoid getting to the point. Like the fancy dinners I sometimes go to now, where they have a million tiny starters instead of just giving us the thing we are there for: the steak. Yet as I sit down to write this appetizer, I feel myself still being pulled toward this need to "make sense" of something. Before I can even think about what I am going to write here, my hands start to type an explanation of all the things this book will figure out.

I start to write long sentences about how *None of the Above* will bring you an understanding of what it means to be neither male nor female. That this book will help you understand how race and transness intersect. That it will help you understand what it means to grow up a faggot in public housing. That it will help you understand why the gender binary in society is harmful. That it will help you understand why anti-trans feminism is flawed. That it will help you understand why the gender binary is racist. That it will help you understand the history of nonbinary experience. That it will help you understand what it means to date as a trans person. That it will help you understand how trans politics will free everyone from gender oppression. That it will help you understand how being trans helped free me. That this book will help you understand.

That this book is about understanding.

That our end goal, after reading it, is comprehension.

That to make sense of something is what makes something successful.

That to understand this book, and in turn me, would stop the violence.

My hands pause. Outside my window, I see a mother put a mask on her child as the child asks why she needs to do that. They repeat this game for about two more minutes. The mother responds with something inaudible from my window, yet it looks like the words "because we have to" or "because COVID," and then the child nods in agreement before becoming bored and taking the mask off a moment later. Each time the child removes the mask, you can see their lack of ability to grasp the world around them. And the mother does not have the words to explain to them either. Understanding feels out of reach.

Only actions seem to make sense. The child carries out the action even if they do not understand it. In writing this book, I feel like that child.

Now, with so much uncertainty around us, even my writing feels questionable. How can any of us pin a fact with certainty to such a movable target? A global pandemic can do so much to rupture your idea of certainty. Yet I am reminded that the world has always been an uncertain project; it has always asked more questions than it has answers to give. It has always left us with inexplicable results. It has always existed between so many lines. However, there is something about writing this book while the world is both metaphorically and literally on fire that makes me think so acutely about discarding old habits—especially the desire to make things neat.

Despite some universals, the year 2020 will be known as many things to different people. What I witnessed was a year of people being uprooted. Things that we thought we could do we no longer could. Moments that we thought were safe became dangerous. Things we believed would always work no longer did. The week I am writing this particular page in September 2020, Beirut has experienced a devastating fire just a month after damaging explosions; a new rule has been announced by the UK government that feels like an impending second lockdown; and there are large areas of California on fire—which many are saying was started in part by a gender-reveal party. I know that when you are reading this, many elections that I am currently worried about will have been held, the planet will be even hotter, and people will still be having gender-reveal parties that burn things down. The chaos is both deeply worrying and calming at the same time.

Nothing feels neat.

Everyone is questioning what will come next. Understanding feels like a far-off reality.

It is as if the world finally looks the way it has always felt to me: inexplicable, contradictory, and consistently in motion. Suddenly, actions, rather than explanations, feel like the clearest thing to hold onto.

I stop myself from looking at the mother and child, who are now several minutes into their back-and-forth.

I try to stop myself from thinking about the wars this world is witnessing. The wars countries are waging against each other, or those of systems against people, or of humans against the planet. I try not to think how apt it is that a large fire devastating lands could have been started by a gender-reveal party—as if gender binaries have not been burning the possibility of life since the moment they began to be enforced. I begin to carry on telling you all the things that this book will help you understand and yet it starts to feel like a lie. The keyboard taps are not light and quick, but heavy and sluggish.

Understanding feels like the most dull and fragile pursuit, like building a beautiful sandcastle on a beach that you know will have a high tide coming in soon enough. Writing all the things I understand, which in turn will help you understand, feels at odds with what is present both in the world and in myself.

The anxiety the whole planet is feeling now reminds me of always checking behind my shoulder to make sure the man following me is not about to attack. Even if you are not affected by the danger now, you know it may be coming. To be gender nonconforming and feminine, or to be trans—or, to put it plainly, to look like someone the world calls a man in a dress—is to know intimately that the world is chaotic, unsettling, and does not make sense. It does not make sense for someone to throw a burger at me in broad daylight and call me a tranny, yet it happens. It does not make sense for people to see it happening and carry on walking, yet it happens. It does not make sense for people to treat you like an animal simply for changing how you present your gender to the world, yet it happens. It does not make sense for people to be afraid of others who have never hurt them, yet they continue to be.

Sense and understanding have never been consistent, so why am I expecting them to hold me securely now?

What can I be sure of? What can I even know?

I know this sounds obtuse, but I'm from a housing project and I'm writing a book, so everything is already fucking obtuse. I regret rushing my prologue for *Burgerz* instead of sitting in the grandness of what it means to write words on a page, so I want to sit in the scale of this.

I cannot start this by making myself small, by telling cisgender people everything I want them to gain from reading this, because that just feels like a replication of our relationship outside this book: presenting my "different" and marginalized story as something they can learn from and about us. An extraction of sorts.

Things are seen as more successful the more they are made comprehensible to the masses (read: the white and not-queer and not-trans). Antiracism books fly off the shelves if they are presented in ways that help (white) people learn comfortably. Feminist-packaged theory is deemed revolutionary if sold in a white, skinny, and highly colorful package. And as I sat down to write this, I had thought that was my goal too. Yet I found myself wondering which people are afforded the ability to question themselves, to interrogate their feelings and write their realities, without the end goal being greater understanding for a certain other group of people. Increasing someone else's understanding may be the consequence of my writing, but to make it the goal seems to empty my writing of something else I desire. I am angry at the me who assumed I was about to serve this function, without even checking if that was what I wanted.

I delete four paragraphs of my efforts to aid cisgender readers in understanding. I try to get the image of a forest fire caused by a gender-reveal party out of my head. I try to not think of the metaphor that falls into my lap with such an image. I try to not romanticize catastrophe.

The truth is: I feel in catastrophe writing this book. I had always dreamed of writing the very book that I just told you this was not going to be. I wanted to write a book that laid out the history of nonbinary identities and how I proudly sat in that history; a book that was like a beacon for the gender-nonconforming life; one that sits outside of all refrains, that screams "genderfucker" into the abyss and refuses to pass in any societal categories.

So many people have privately messaged me to say it is "inspiring to have a trans person in public who does not look like a man or a woman," and I secretly wanted to write a book for all of them. To create a bold manifesto of arguments for the people who refuse to fit within gender. For the Black genderfuckers. For those of us who check "none of the above" on forms. When I decided to write this book, I felt so sure in my own understanding of self that I was ready to lay out the reality of my existence so someone else could understand me.

Yet I can't help but think about how, by the time I finish this book, it will not just be the world that has changed, but also myself. All this time alone with myself, in isolation from the world but consequently with my body and self, has brought into greater focus than ever my relationship to my body. There is a nagging in my chest each day, and not just one that tells me I need to write this book, but another one that tells me: maybe I need to start making changes to myself. Maybe I need to transition alongside the world.

The first thing I did with the advance from this book was march to a clinic and start the process of laser hair removal on my face. By the time this goes to print, the cosmetic surgeries I've planned to make my face look more "feminine" may have been successful, so I will need a new author photo. Who knows if I will even be using the same name in casual conversation to refer to myself? So many of these changes in both the world and me were unexpected. A few years ago, I could not imagine what a pandemic would look like, yet I could also not ever imagine wanting to change my face. The nineteen-year-old me proudly vandalizing a club toilet with "bearded sissy and proud" would curse the me who just sat through excruciating pain each month to make sure I never have to shave again. The twenty-year-old me who answered, "Fuck you, I'm something beyond" to strangers shouting, "Is that a man or a woman?" on the street now has a niggling urge to be able to glide past without a stare or a look. The twenty-two-year-old me who contemplated getting my pronouns (they/them) tattooed on my hand now quietly smiles when someone accidentally calls me "she."

Here I am wondering if my body and its desires are coming into conflict with my theory, wondering if the tattoo on my left wrist, a Venn diagram with an X in the intersection, that resembles the pride of not conforming, suddenly becomes void when I am considering transitioning to look more like *them*. I feel that I am growing into a contradiction of myself and wonder how I can write a book about everything I want you to understand when there is so much about myself and the world that I am so far from grasping. Am I wanting to make these changes for myself, or is this a result of exhaustion? Is this just an aim to be understood?

I acutely remember Amber, a trans woman in her late thirties, who has been coming to my shows for the last five years, saying to me in Cambridge after a performance of *Burgerz*: "I'm glad you exist. You are everything I'm too afraid to be." And as I sit here thinking about myself, understanding, changing—all I can think of are Amber's words. About whether I have become tired of being the thing everyone is afraid to be.

And I realize that, as I try to think about myself and the world, and all that is changing around both, the phrases that people have said to me refuse to budge. As I sit in the chair to have my stubble burned off for the third time, I cannot forget the first time someone said, "You would be sexier if you shaved." Or, as I hover over the prescription for estrogen, I think of a friend telling me, "If you continue not to conform, you will always be excluded." So many phrases have been uttered to me and have clung to me ever since.

Even as your body or your politics or your world may change, a phrase can last a lifetime—waiting to resurface.

And I have had a lot of things said to me.

When you are someone who falls outside of categories in so many ways, a lot of things *are* said to you. You often become a place to hold other people's confusion. You become a site for their internal process to become external. Your lack of ability to fit into the boxes they are trying to place you in provokes an almost word-vomit response. In order to survive, it is impossible to give time to every phrase said to you: if you honored and gave space to every time someone called you a faggot on the street, you would never get home. If you gave breath to every time someone asked,

"Where are you really from?" then you would stay lost. You have no choice but to move on.

That is, until you sit down to write a book, notionally about all the things you want people to understand about being you, where *you* means trans. Where *you* means neither male or female. Where *you* means being Black yet also mixed race. Where *you* means being raised by an immigrant African American mother in the UK, knowing that, although they call you Black, you are also Filipino, and British, and French, and Mexican. Where *you* means poor and somehow still alive in this country. Where *you* means someone who has never fit in, yet is now wondering if it will be easier to conform. Where *you* means someone who has endured newspapers attacking them, passersby staring at them, but who also receives deep and profound love from communities they once did not know existed. In that *you*, it feels there are too many moving parts to seek something as conditional as understanding.

Yet through all these moving parts, identities, and frameworks, I hear phrases being spoken to me so clearly, phrases that can only be said to the *you* that I am, because I am all the things aforementioned: I do not fit. I hear phrases that can only be said to me because I am all the things I thought I wanted to get others to understand.

And I realize that maybe those phrases are a way into myself that starts not with an explanation, not with an aim to understand, but with an experience rooted in action and feeling.

So, in this book, I am going to tell you about phrases that have been said to me in the course of my life.

Phrases that, as I try to understand who I am, seem to be sticking in my head. Phrases that, as I and the world change, seem to be staying with me. Phrases that feel like both shouts and whispers, hugs and punches—phrases that are routinely said to people like me. Phrases that also can *only* be said to someone like me. Phrases from lovers, from hecklers, from shopkeepers, from friends, from the press. Phrases that do not aim for an understanding. Phrases that I will repeat and explore in these pages, to make a record of the fact that I was here.

As we spend more and more time alone, in isolation and away from our former routines, I am struck by how these phrases have stayed with me, despite all the ways I have changed.

They are phrases that have withstood my tests of time.

They are phrases that will immortalize the experiences of those who are

*None of the above.*

# The Sea

## I

Sometimes I stand by the edge where the ocean meets the beach, and look out into the sea, so I can see something that does not have an end.

I often get asked what my gender feels like,

and I want to say: it is more like, what do I wish it could feel like?

I wish it could feel like this moment.

Like it does not have a beginning or an end. Like you cannot see where it starts or stops. Like it just continues to exist, or not exist.

Like it is a vast space of nothingness in one wave, and holds so much in the next.

Sometimes I stand by the edge where the ocean meets the beach, and look out into the sea, so I can feel like something that does not have an end.

## II

Cis people ask me what my gender feels like, and that never allows me to say what my gender really is. My gender is something stopped halfway through.

A badly formatted tape-to-CD conversion, not meeting its full potential.

The second character in a video game, without levels, no up or down. It is an unfinished—

A body of water, potential to do so much, yet eventually bottled.

Sometimes I stand by the edge where the ocean meets the beach, and look out into the sea, that looks out over my gender, that pours over my body, and makes me feel like nothing.

# 1

## "So when did you know?"

I sit in the doctor's office.

He asks, "So when did you know?"

I say, "Always," because I've heard simplicity gets results.

o

It is one phrase that has spanned across my lifetime. No matter what setting, country, or occasion—it remains undefeatable. Like a cockroach that refuses to disappear, it doesn't care which part of my life I am in. It will always emerge:

"So when did you know?"

People always ask me this, or if I am not around, they will be sure to ask my mother, or a friend, or even a teacher that I haven't seen in years—"So when did Travis . . . *you know?*" The "you" and "know" will come with verbalized italics. If an emoji could appear out of thin air, it would be the eyes darting to the side of the room accompanied by a vague hand gesture, as if to say: so when was it clear Travis would become a cross-dressing deviant who is straying from God's path?

Childhood is always an interesting topic to raise if you want to get to know someone. Often a telltale sign of a relationship deepening is learning about your partner's embarrassing school story or when they first broke the law. I can tell I am maybe entering the terrifying process of falling in love with someone when, after sex, instead of rushing to put my pants on and have a cigarette, we are suddenly recounting parts of our childhood—the good and the hard bits alike. This fascination is natural; it makes sense. We want to learn more about the people we are drawn to, and we know how much the past clings to us all. Like cat hair that sheds onto new clothes, it can't be shaken off. It makes sense that, to learn more and become closer to them, you would want to understand all the cogs that created the person in front of you—the one who has to leave the main light on all day, even if they are not in the room, to keep the dark at bay. Learning these idiosyncrasies usually comes with time, but in my experience of being visibly gender nonconforming and trans—like with many social expectations and norms—my existence supersedes any agreed social contract of how people are supposed to act. My perceived transgression approves all of theirs.

Of course, humans are naturally curious, but I find British ways of communicating to be crowded with social pleasantries and forced "politeness"—an investment in never rocking the boat or being seen as out of line. Asking any form of direct question at a British dinner table can cause waves of disapproving murmurs for months. But present that same dinner table with someone who is visibly gender nonconforming, wearing a dress, with a bit of a five-o'clock shadow coming through, and all of those manners privately bought at some elitist institution disappear. "So when did you know?" becomes their version of weather talk or asking what you do for a living. Suddenly, the intimacy of your childhood and memories becomes expected fodder for the public forum—not just for those you may regret having in your bed later. People want to know, often within the first handshake or moment you sit down, whether you were always like this, what your parents think, the defining moment you knew, and when you first tried on the red lipstick and dress from your mother's closet (even if you, in fact, never did). Perhaps what is even more terrifying is, for a long time, I felt I owed every question an answer.

○

"So when did you know, uh . . . ?" asks a donor to a very popular LGBT+ charity in the UK at a private dinner celebrating volunteers. The "uh" is followed by a grand gesture of her hand, pointing up and down to my outfit and makeup.

I take a sharp breath to prepare my answer.

"Well, when I was around three years old my mother took me to the doctor, because I had not spoken my first word yet. She was worried. I was her second child and my older brother couldn't shut up, making full sentences by the age of three . . ."

The rich white donor lady leans in. A parasite to blood, my sob story is her vitamin, supplementing the four-course meal she has not touched. She nods, as if to say, *Go on, don't stop, tell me how, exactly, you knew.*

Seeing that this story is working, I continue.

"So my mother took me to the doctor. The doctor inspected me, and did hearing tests and more, to check if there was a problem with any of my senses. He realized I was not deaf, so then he started to look inside my throat, to check if it was anything to do with my vocal cords." She is nodding ferociously at this point. I can tell she is waiting for the meat of this story to be served, enjoying the picture I am painting, but mostly eagerly awaiting the reveal she came for.

"And then, just as the doctor had given up on finding why I could not speak, as he was packing up his bag, I turned around and I opened my mouth and said my very first words. And do you know what they were?"

She shakes her head. Saliva builds around her mouth as she awaits the fruits of her inquiry.

"I opened my mouth, age three, and said my first words: 'Doctor, I am actually a cross-dressing, gender-nonconforming deviant.' And that is how we all knew something was different about me."

It takes a moment for the rich white donor of an LGBT+ charity, who had not even asked how I was before asking how I knew, to realize that of course the story is false. She lets out a high-pitched staccato laugh, clearly frustrated by the long setup for my story and that it did not give her what she wanted. I smile quietly, as if I have just told a truly harrowing and revealing tale. I then ask if she can pass the gravy, and wonder for a moment if she will later process why her question provoked such a response from me.

Because of the frequency with which I am asked when I "knew," I try to have a quick response ready in my armory.

I am not always at a fancy dinner or have that amount of time and energy to string a delicate story together for my own amusement. Sometimes I cannot find the humor in such an affronting question from a stranger. Sometimes I need a punchier line to diffuse the affront, something along the lines of being raised by a pack of wolves who only spoke to me in quotes from Judith Butler books, or that I was adopted by a wholesome group of trans feminist lesbians who slowly but thoroughly converted me to my gender deviation. Most of the time, however, the interrogator is too engrossed in their own knee-jerk questioning to notice any hint of sarcasm on my part. Or they believe that in my transitioning, I also lost all ability to have a sense of humor.

For the purpose of this book, though, I actually want to know the real answer to this question. Me writing the words on a page and you reading them is not the same as the rich white lady posing the question two minutes after meeting me, or the primary care doctor or the long-distance relative I see for the first time in fifteen years doing the same. The missing ingredient in the aforementioned scenarios is choice, *opting in* to the conversation rather than reacting to it. All those years of being asked the question so often without choice means that I want to find the answer for myself from a place of control.

There are many things oppression and its side effects take from you, and one of them, I believe, is an easier access to your truth: if it is so regularly questioned, sometimes it proves harder to find when no one is around. It's challenging to understand if I have a distinctive memory of when I "knew" because of the performance around this question, but I often try to find one, so that even as I palm off interrogations with quick-witted jokes, I can know the answer for myself, deep down.

*So, Travis, when* did *you know?*

I try to find a memory, something that tells me I am certain, that I am definitely who I say I am—but I cannot find one. It's not simply that I cannot find a memory that makes me sit up straight in a moment of recognition, a moment of "that must be it, here is my defining trans moment, everything else now makes sense," but more that I can't find a memory untainted by the heavy lens of this questioning.

The forced inquisition from cisgender people through-out my life has left my own ability to know what is and is not real harder to grasp. When I am not fighting to explain myself to someone else and am looking for my own answers, I suddenly worry I cannot find the truth. When a part of you is so heavily scrutinized and interrogated, in order to protect yourself you have to present it as immutable. Doing so, however, leaves you without some of the flexibility and openness needed for reflection when you are on your own.

I want to know if I can find my transness when no one is looking for it.

What if I do not know? What if what they are saying is true? What if I am just a male body of genitalia and bones that is in a prolonged game of dressing up? What if what the papers say about us is correct? If I cannot even find the moment of when I knew, then how will anyone else believe me? What if I am not really "trans enough" after all?

I think of other people I have heard speak about their moment of knowing, how they say their parents recall how they cried whenever they were in the wrong clothing. I think of my friends who had similar early experiences, where their first words to a doctor may not have been those I comically made up for the lady at the dinner table, but their cries may as well have said the same thing. I think of an article I read by another trans person speaking of the indescribable pain of knowing innately they were not in the body they were supposed to be, how their childhood was plagued with the consistent reminder of being told they were a gender they were not. And I draw a blank. I cannot pin this reality onto mine. I can see discomfort in my memories, but the source never feels like it is within me, only imposed by someone else.

That's not to say I'm not aware of so many trans people who also do not have this narrative; I know trans women who transitioned in their late fifties and cannot pinpoint defining moments of realization. I know and am aware of the ways in which our identities span multiple realities. But when the specifics of my nonbinary identity are constantly questioned, I cannot help but hold onto the idea that I should have an answer to this question that feels more robust; that feels unmovable in a sea of external pressures and doubt; that tells the world—but also me—that I am real, and am what I say I am. If I can figure out when I knew, I can walk with the confidence of always having known, something that cements me in my belief.

So, Travis, when *did* you know?

Maybe it was a collection of memories and moments, like a constellation of lightbulbs turning on, that eventually amounted to this. I think about the house I grew up in and one of my earliest memories there. I was raised in a red-brick house in government housing in a neglected suburb of Bristol, the kind of public housing that looks like every other photo of public housing you have seen; truly nothing that felt out of the ordinary. A lot of houses that all looked the same, a grassy square in the middle of them with no streetlights, and a corner shop that was holding up the army of families lining up for a pint of milk. The monotony of it may have been part of its charm, but I think you can only have that perspective seeing it from the outside, or with hindsight. Escape feels like a prerequisite to finding balance when talking about the housing project. To be on the inside was to feel like you were waking up in a large maze of bricks without an exit.

In one of those houses—number 38 to be precise—lived

my mother, my older brother, and a four-year-old me. Although the house was cold, bare in its furniture, and had cracks in its ceilings from deterioration that the government had yet to deal with—our family was the opposite of our material reality. We were warm, loud, and most definitely excessive: three very strong-minded people who made a home full of belly laughs, lots of singing, shouting, and plenty of talking. Life was not quiet in our house. Poverty is always a loud force, but we shouted back just as loudly, refusing to let the sound of scarcity win.

If you put your ear up to the wall, you could have a listen . . .

o

"Introducing . . . Travis Alabanza!" says the German lodger, Hangwolf, who, though primarily there to pay our food bills, develops into a brief but important and loving figure in the house. A tall, statuesque man who fits into the structure of our unit, almost as if there was a gap left from a father, still warm for Hangwolf to walk into.

"Hangwolf, you have to introduce me with the name of the song I'm singing, you can't just say my name!" I say offstage (which, at this point in my life, means the living room).

"Singing his new song, 'All You Need Is a Shoe,' introducing . . . Travis Alabanza!"

And the rest is history. That is how the 1999 record-breaking hit "All You Need Is a Shoe" was born, smashing all previous chart records, and the royalties clearing every Alabanza out of generational cycles of poverty forevermore. Or at least, that is the kind of energy I brought to my debut when I performed it in the kitchen to my mother, older brother, and our German lodger, Hangwolf. I may not have known why at that tender age, but the gusto matched the cause: even at the age of four I could sense that intentionality was key to a good performance. My small feet shuffling in my mother's heels as I marched unknowingly into each gender-nonconforming child's cliché memory, focused only on performing the best rendition of the song yet.

The song lyrics were simple: the only line to the hit single "All You Need Is a Shoe" was that of the title. If you want to sing it as you read this, you simply pick any tune you like and sing those words with extreme enthusiasm. It does not matter if the next time you sing it, the tune is not the same, or if the rhythm is off; the magic is more about the experience than the execution.

It didn't matter how four-year-old me performed the song; the applause was rapturous each time. Mum cheered for an encore no matter how many times she had heard it, our German lodger Hangwolf hummed the song to himself in the shower, even my stoic brother released a smile when it was sung.

Like most repeated performances, over time, the function shifted and the natural impulses that created it made way for more overthought intentions. Soon I would sing the hit song not because I wanted to but because I knew it would make Hangwolf smile, or even my usually serious brother laugh. Four-year-old me became acquainted early with the burden of creating a commercial success.

Dreams of grandeur or projections of pop-star life onto four-year-old me aside, when I think about how I "knew"—where the knowing means transgression, an uncomfortableness with being "boy," a hint at the future deviance I would inhabit—maybe it all started with this performance of "All You Need Is a Shoe" in my kitchen in a housing project in the suburbs of Bristol.

Provide us with the magnifying glass of perspective and we can hold our memories under it for inspection. In this one, we see the signs that this was when we all knew the kid would be "different": the knowing smile from my mum to the German lodger, the flamboyance in my arm gestures as I performed the song, and, most obviously, a four-year-old devoting the first year of their artistic career to a song about longing for a red high-heeled shoe. Subtlety has never been a virtue of mine.

Surely this was how I knew? If I were telling this story at a dinner party in response to another person asking me the question yet again, I would receive full marks. The rich white lady donor (for it would inevitably be another one) would be lapping up every word. You see, there are the clear signifiers that link this story to the mainstream perception of trans identity, particularly those of us assigned male at birth: the high-heeled shoe and the performativity of the song effortlessly blends with the public imagination of how all transfeminine people discover our gender. Combined with the quirkiness of a hunky German lodger, this story, when told right, often results in a sea of smiles, unthreatened nods, and a calmness washing over the room. A calmness that is specific to liberal cisgender people feeling comfortable again because they have you all figured out: now they know how you *knew*.

Yet actually, when I look more closely at this memory, none of that feels certain to me. I can see the joy so vividly on my face. The kind of joy I recognize now as that which comes from the perfect symphony of being yourself, of others celebrating that, and of being in a place of safety. I can touch my curiosity in the memory. If I look close enough into my own eyes, just after the song finishes, I can tell I am smiling not just about the soon-to-be hit single—but also about the discovery of something else. I know that the joy I found in thinking about that high-heeled shoe was real, but none of that led to a knowing. In fact, *knowing* feels like the exact opposite of what encompassed that memory, because I was too busy *doing*. There was not a surrounding conversation because I was just allowed to be present: present in action, without speculation.

So to give that as an answer to when I first "knew" feels like an addition made in hindsight, which becomes so much less about the integrity of the memory or question and more about the comfort in finding the answer. It helps me realize that so often when I've scrambled for a memory to talk about "when I knew," it was to pacify an obsession from the other person rather than an actual desire of my own to know. If we accept that gender nonconformity and transness are things the world and the individual aim to stamp out and erase, then I start to see "So when did you know?" as a question to make sense of a blip in the matrix. Almost as if the impulse to ask is an attempt to calm their disbelief that I can still exist. I do hear the question more often at formal events, when I'm rubbing shoulders with the traditions of society, and it is often asked by the "well-intentioned" holder of tradition in the room. "So when did you know?" becomes a way to reinstate an order of events, an order that gender nonconformity disrupts.

I think of the time a police officer in the United States asked me, "How did you know?" as part of his attempt at small talk, after stopping to search me near a restaurant in

Boston. Or the time a director at an audition blurted it out as his first question, after I delivered a monologue about a boy missing his father who was away at war. No matter how pure the intention may be, every time I hear the phrase, I remember all the moments it was uttered on impulse, without thought. It makes me wonder what power lies in being visibly gender nonconforming, that no matter where you may be, your mere existence causes social rules to snap, professionalism to collapse, and conversation to be completely dictated by people's fascination. So powerful that you do not just stop traffic with your looks—you also control tongues.

Yet despite how many times I have had to withstand the inappropriate questioning, I still wish I could pinpoint an answer that felt honest, even if just for the rare time it is asked from a place of safety and comfort, even if it is just so I know myself.

I replied to the casting director, "When I played a witch in a school play; I was thirteen." He nodded, as if that was an answer that made sense to him, so he could move on. He looked at the figure in front of him, saw the shadow poking through my jaw, and could draw the lines of where a witch once was, or could be.

I think about the memory of that school play now, remembering how I felt when I asked my drama teacher if I could play the witch in the school show. How quick she was to say yes, how everyone else paused, wondering if I was serious. How the moment I put on the dress, heels, and tights for the role, I felt a sense of confidence I had not before. How the moment I went out onto the stage, I experienced instantly the comfort and celebration we have with gender nonconformity when it is placed in the realm of performance. The football boys who were there to watch the popular girls in my drama class came ready to laugh and point at me, but instead laughed involuntarily at how well I fulfilled the role. Maybe this was it. Maybe becoming the witch was how I knew I was trans, as if *witch* and *transfeminine* were synonyms I was already acutely aware of.

But as I write this, nothing about the memory feels like a knowing. "Knowing" should feel like the remaining jigsaw piece, found after months and months of searching for it, slotting into place. I am so aware of what "always knowing" something feels like, and this is not it—all these memories I can use to prove that I always knew, that I was always there, that this was always a thing. But if I take away the need to prove and defend, I am just left with the joy, the freedom, the feelings. There is not a knowing in sight, just a clear release in being left alone to *be*. No moment I can pinpoint reveals an innate knowing of my transness, rather, each is just another example of how I am responded to by the outside world.

Okay, okay, but when did you *know*? Well, maybe I never did know.

I do not think I am innately trans. Let me get that out of the way first. I do not think I was born this way. I am not convinced that I have known inside of me, since the moment of conception, that I was destined to change anything specifically about me. I am not sure I was destined to feel repulsed at the thought of calling myself a man, or to wear dresses, red heels, and Mac red lipstick. (I still don't think red lipstick looks that good on me.)

Before the skeptics aim to use this as proof for any theory they may have about us: this is not to say that I do not think I am trans. I am sure of it. If trans means to be something other than the gender you were forcibly assigned at birth, then deck the halls and give me the ghastly colored trans flag: I am surely trans. I am so trans that when someone refers to me as a "he" in passing, I have to remind myself that they could possibly be talking about me. I am so trans that I have about twenty-five different names I call my genitalia, yet have still just landed on the word _____. I am so trans that I thought about having my pronouns tattooed on my wrists—yet am trans enough to know that is a distasteful idea. I am trans. This chapter, or book really, is not about convincing myself (or you) of that fact—I would have needed that book when I was seventeen. I am no longer interested in trying to prove such an unshakable fact. It is a fact that I have learned will not go away. It is a fact that is simply a part of me, much like my passion for performing, or my eternal need to binge-watch reality TV shows (although the latter two cause much less commotion). However, just because something is true does not mean that it must always have been so. Meaning, I think I am trans because I exist in this century, right now in this time, but just like years and decades and places move, I think, so could my transness. If I existed a century ago, on the streets of New York, would I be agonizing about these words seeking to define me, or would I instead just be walking, heels in hand, as I'm secretly placing them in my bag? Or what if I existed four hundred years from now, and somehow the world was still above water, and no one was throwing burgers or fists or knives at us—would I still be trans?

I believe my transness is a reactionary fact, not an innate one. I am trans because the world made me so, not because I was born different. I am trans because the systems the world operates through force me to be so, not because of genetics. I am trans because of you, not because of me. I did not always know, because I once imagined a world where I would not have to know. More than this, I believe that others may only be so very cis because the world is forcing the same reaction from them too. That my reaction to declare transness is similar to the cisgender men and women running away from any chance of something else. When the gender binary is created so harshly, all it forces from us are strong reactions— because it eradicates any chance of a calm self-discovery. Transness is held to a higher scrutiny, so we are seen as the performative choice or reaction, rather than as living proof of the reactionary ways the gender binary makes us live. We, rather than the gender binary itself, are seen as unnatural. So much of the narrative around LGBTQIA+ identities, especially those more marginalized, such as transness, rely on us to state that we were innately born this way in order for us to be accepted. We "cannot help who we are," so therefore deserve to be protected. Safety is conditional on our innate difference. We need a discovery moment that is clear as day, that highlights the unchangeable reality that we exist.

Yet I think this obsession with asserting innate knowing onto transness is to comfort Michelle at the dinner table, rather than to really try and understand us. It places the identity of the other person, the non-trans questioner, into a passive rather than an active state. Muted, almost. If you make it all about the way I was born, or an immovable innate fact, then the identity in question has nothing to do with you and the responsibility falls solely on me. Then transness becomes all about the individual—how they were born, what genetics they may or may not have, how they are the anomaly to the rule—and less about the systems and circumstances that may have impacted the way they view themselves and their gender. It becomes all about how I gained knowledge around an immovable fact, rather than how cisgender and Western binary thinking made gender two immovable posts to define myself within. It works as a way to make us, the born-this-way-can't-change-us trans people, more understandable—and therefore respectable.

When I think about the moment I hobbled in heels out onto the school stage as a witch, dress tight around my knees and stockings ripped on purpose, it was not an experience that felt particularly trans. Rather, when I think about that moment, if I try to find any moment of knowing, all I can do is think of you—where *you* means the boys watching in the audience. Before I laid my mascara-slathered eyes on the crowd, all I felt within myself was an ease, a power, a joy— all of which can and do exist in transness—but I do not think transness was there. My transness, I believe, might have always required a "you" in order to show itself. Maybe I only know I am trans because you make it impossible for me not to be.

The boys' eyes in the audience. The first five minutes as they try to decide whether to heckle or clap. The whispers under the breath. The questioning that follows the moment I leave the stage: "So what are you?" that later turns to "So when will you stop doing this?" that still later becomes "So when did you know?" It feels impossible for my transness not to be born out of reactions, when I live in a world in which gender nonconformity is seen as deviant, causing others to become agents, policing us. My gender, like all of ours, does not exist in a silo away from everyone else's. Much like a boy believes he should not cry because he has never seen his father do it, or a man throws punches because that is what he has seen his brothers do, gender and our experience of it only comes into knowing around other people. Why must our transness be exempt from that? Why does it have to be something we are born into, in order to make it valid and understandable to you? Why must empirical proof be a prerequisite for care?

If I was born this way, then you do not need to change.

If I was born this way, then it has nothing to do with you.

If I was born this way, then transness can continue to be distanced.

## "So when did you know?"

As I sit across from the doctor in his office, trying to start the process of getting hormones through the National Health System, he pauses before his next question. Like the lady who lasered the hair off my chin last week, he asks me if I always knew. I say yes, and I tell him the story of shuffling in my mother's red shoes as I sang a song devoted to high heels. He laughs and takes a note, asks me if there was any other "clear sign," and I tell him about when I played a witch in the school play. He nods. He likes that story. It confirms everything he's ever thought about us.

I think about him writing down his notes, and how they will become a form of archive of my existence. They will be passed on to the next doctor I may see; maybe he will break confidentiality and tell his wife abstractly about me after work. Or the nurse will see the notes and use the information as a way to seem more progressively liberal to her extended family at Christmas, my notes becoming the quick conversation buffer to ensure her Gen Z relative knows she really is on the right side of everything that has existed ever. This version of myself I gave him becomes my origin story.

Trans stories are so washed out of historical archives that some of the only records we have are the responses we give to the medical system controlled by gatekeepers. Doctors' notes. Justifications. Pleadings. And when the doctors ask us questions about ourselves, we have to limit our story in order to reach our next stage in transition; the archive never, therefore, holds us in full. We give the answer we know will work, that we all know deep down is not what we want to say, so the complicated truth is never spoken out loud. Which, if I answered honestly, would probably go something like this:

*I do not think I do know, Doctor. I cannot tell you the moment the penny dropped. There was not a singular turn of a page that led me to this. When I think about the memories I just shared with you, I cannot be certain, but when I think of the me within them— all I know is that they were free. They were not thinking about who this meant they were, or who they definitely were not; rather, they were just existing. Yet something happened. I grew up and became tired. The world forces me to justify who I am. When I have been punished every single time I stepped outside of a box, I had to start thinking about who I may be. If my body fell in the middle of the woods, and there was no one around to call it a tranny, I'm not sure if I would hate it. I'm not sure I would be aching for my beard to go, if I didn't constantly feel illegible as the person I am now, if that illegibility did not lead to material danger. Who knows if I would be trying to soften my face, if a hard face in a tight dress did not lead to a burger being thrown at me?*

*Doctor, I cannot possibly tell you when I first knew. All I can see are the countless moments you and the world continually let me know that not knowing was never an option. That I needed to know in order for you to feel comfortable. That if I was not this, I had to be that, otherwise I would continually be punished. I do not think this feeling, this discomfort in my body, exists without* you. In fact, I think it is created by you. Maybe if none of you were here, I also would not be. But, Doctor, that does not really matter, because you are here. Which means I am certain something has to change. Because I am tired, and I know this is not working. And my autonomy over my body, to solve an issue that I believe you may have helped cause, really should have nothing to do with you. Yet because my dysphoria and healthcare require your approval, it now has everything to do with you as well.

And respectfully, Doctor, when or whether I always knew is not what is keeping me up at night. It is not what they ask before they look or shout.

It is just a question, the answer to which leads us both nowhere. And Doctor, I am here,

Because I am trying to go somewhere.

# 2

## "But I mean, *real* trans."

I open up to a friend about the fact that I am thinking of starting hormones. My friend nods and hugs me.

She says, "I wondered when you were going to start this whole thing for real."

o

Feeling like an imposter is not a new sensation for me. I've read (and written) enough blog posts on imposter syndrome to know that whoever is reading this has felt it too—a lack of belonging is not an uncommon feeling. Whether it be the workplace, our places of education, the groups we identify within, or our bodies, a common thread is that this world will make many of us feel like visitors. Often, when I look at the moments I have felt like an imposter, they boil down to an order being set and me not fitting within it. There are rules, clear or subtle, that the space is governed by—and I am either in direct conflict with these rules or trailing behind them. Sometimes I have the strength to push past those regulations, and other times I do not.

When I attended university for two years, I was filled with newfound doubt about the way I spoke. This was not an innate doubt I had always felt but one that appeared as

I entered a place with a new set of rules around speech. I had never noticed that I had anything close to a Bristolian-sounding accent, until a professor asked me where in the UK I was from. When I said Bristol, she quickly said, "I thought so!" without missing a beat, yet with a facial expression that looked as if she could smell my dinner from last night still on my breath. The quickness and tone suggested a negative connotation. I found it odd, since in the more working-class area I grew up in within Bristol, my voice didn't stand out as particularly Bristolian—yet here, within the frame of an old and rotting university institution, my accent was spotted within a second. A reminder that these things are often situational.

I think this took place the same week that I was stuck in a lunchtime conversation with other freshmen who were bonding over their rankings of the best places to ski in Europe. I remember one with mousy brown hair and a Ralph Lauren jumper (yes, there was only one of them in this group—by 2013, the posh girls had started wearing Adidas) who turned to me with a look of proffered inclusion as if to say, *You can join in too: tell me your favorite place to ski.* I paused and replied, "Bristol has lots of hills, so when it snows it's the ultimate ski resort, babes." We imposters often know how to disarm with a quick joke. Let them laugh loud enough that they forget you may be out of place.

These experiences alone did not cause a collapse of my confidence—I would hope to be more resilient than that. It was more that, over time, similar scenarios helped show me where I fit or did not fit among the other students. When certain experiences are established as norms and the expectation, repeatedly deviating from them is something you notice in yourself. Starting my first acting job while never having acted in a Shakespeare play. Becoming a resident artist at the Tate Gallery, but never having gone to art school and having to ask what "having a practice" meant on the first day. Not being white, and living in a country with a history of colonizing lands populated by people of color. Being an imposter is not a new sensation to me.

## "But I mean, *real* trans."

I cannot always detach from those feelings, and even when I can, sometimes it is harder than others. I have not magically escaped feelings of imposture surrounding class within British society, or what it means to be Black and mixed race in a country like Britain. Even in writing this book, analyzing every sentence, I am loudly reminded who is told they can write books and who is not. Beyond the long tradition of publishing being a space for the highly educated, the rich, and the white, I also mean specifically who can write books about gender, and even more so, transness. One scroll on Twitter makes it clear the types of people who are allowed to analyze their gender and the effects of it on the world: namely white, middle-class, and if not cisgender, they must definitely have a PhD or be trying to get one. Not a university dropout like me, eh? We are allowed to have upbeat, anecdotal conversations, but analyze a word or a sentence? Who gave us permission to do such a thing?

Those feelings of imposture have been incredibly loud with every word I've written so far, yet what I mean by detaching is that I can go hours or days or weeks without external reminders of those feelings. So when they arise again, I can zoom out and remind myself of other truths.

Even when it comes to race, I find that, although I know and am sure of the way racism is playing out in the day-to-day situations I find myself in, I am not walking out onto the street and being reminded of it by strangers every second of every day. Of course, this is in no small part down to the fact that I am not dark-skinned, meaning my proximity to white-ness will shield me from certain racialized daily aggressions. And I am sure the thoughts and comments still happen, but not to the point where they are stopping me from going to get milk at the shop.

The same cannot be said of my gender nonconformity. The local shop in the last place I lived in London refused to speak to or serve me and my three visibly gender-noncon-forming roommates. We had to go to another shop. Being visibly trans, consistently read as failing at either male or female gender, means I am lucky to walk outside and not be shouted at, or laughed at, or filmed within the space of a day. This is not an exaggeration: it's a mere fact for those of us who walk through the streets and dare to be gender nonconforming (and feminine) in public. I believe it is the constant and consistent ridicule, violence, or challenge placed on gender nonconformity—coupled with the media's and other people's interrogations, alongside my own—that make the process of what I call "zooming out" from feel-ings of imposture harder for me. I know that my race and my class impact the ways my gender nonconformity is read and policed, that these things influence each other, but I can tell when it is the fact that I am wearing a dress with leg hair showing that has motivated a man to film me on a busy street in broad daylight. We can always tell. Like it is the last nail in the coffin.

The proximity and consistency of the violence and

interrogation others direct at my gender nonconformity make my own feelings of imposture greater. I do not want to feel as obsessed with my gender and my body as others are—yet I have forgotten how to be anything other than hyper-aware of it. I know I do not want to feel like an imposter in my body for the rest of my life, yet I am also not sure how to change that. And even if I am internally figuring out how I personally will solve this, in regard to gender presentation, there are material dangers and consequences for this lack of surety about the specific gender nonconformity within my transness. You cannot work out your gender in public unless you are prepared to navigate how the world punishes you for this.

When you are specifically gender nonconforming, and that gender nonconformity is seen as an intentional and permanent fixture, there are a whole host of assumptions made about you—not just in the wider world but also within your own community. This questioning and the assumptions made about you are not just hurtful; they also have material and physical consequences to your lived experience. We are structurally impacted by this lack of understanding: if people do not understand our experiences as gender-nonconforming people, our access to services to support us will be hugely affected, as well as our access to solidarity and empathy. To be seen as an imposter within gender is to straddle precarity in public and private spaces. In public, the power of a binary and transphobic state means it is currently not possible to register legally as neither male nor female in the UK, so your forms, legal documents, and medical records still must situate you within one of the binary options. There is a huge gap in material support for those of us outside of the binary.

Beyond this, a lack of understanding of us and our needs by a cisgender culture results in us falling through the cracks in terms of changing policies and public attitude toward us. If a population views those of us outside the binary as "women lite" or "men lite," and tailors their support or treatment to whichever gender they feel we most closely occupy, they miss out on the specific ways in which violence is inflicted toward gender-nonconforming nonbinary people. An example of this is harassment and the recording and reporting of it. Often, it is those who are visibly gender nonconforming, particularly those still seen as a "man in a dress," who are deemed dangers to society, specifically to women and girls. However, if you walk outside appearing to the world as a "man in a dress," you will often receive not just threats or actual acts of sexual and physical violence from men but also harassment and violence from women. You will often be filmed without your consent by children. But then who can we as gender-nonconforming people turn to for support in these moments of attack, if each group in public is also a potential threat? Because a cisgender culture ignores and eliminates those outside the binary, we are not only not believed regarding our potential to experience harm, but we are often demonized and seen as the ones responsible for causing that harm.

In private—where *private* means between friends, among others of the queer and trans community—to be outside the binary, to be trans, is sometimes to be met with a lack of solidarity. There is a particular gatekeeping surrounding the word *trans* within our own community, whereby it is deemed a legitimate identity only if you are medicalized. Comments are made that the nonbinary, or those of us seen as not attempting to "pass," are not "real" in our transness and genders.

40

Although the intracommunity discrimination comes without the structural power of a binary and transphobic state, it is still hard to heal from. It's a vivid reminder that to be neither, within a binary world, is to sacrifice both state and sometimes community protection, to learn quickly how solidarity is conditional. The solidarity you receive is dependent on others' judgment of your attempt at gender.

o

"But, I mean, *real* trans—you've not had any surgeries done." I was with a friend in one of those pubs that feel like they shouldn't still exist. Not in a bad way—I'm so glad they do still exist. Only in these kinds of pubs, whose bricks have somehow held firm long enough not to be smashed by incoming apartment buildings and yoga moms moving in next door, could you witness a group of soccer players, some goth art students, the marketing crew from ASOS, and a bunch of queer and trans artists all having the same watered-down pint. It's a place that actually makes you want to use the dreaded D-word (diversity) because it genuinely feels apt. Even in this mixed-up space, no one was fighting, or at least if there was ever a fight, I didn't see it. Of course, only the locals would be invited to the private party.

My friend and I were not fighting either, and we were not about to, even as she looked me dead in the eye and said, "But, I mean, *real* trans." I let the comment slide by me. Not even in some moral-high-ground way, but more, I think, because subconsciously I agreed with her. Deep down, what she was saying did not seem like a big deal, let alone wrong. Just one sentence in the midst of thousands slurred that night six years ago, which, when your days are spent thinking endlessly about your gender and body, is a very long time. A lot changes in six years, and I find that, in discovering new parts of my gender and how I relate to it, phrases that once washed right past me resurface and cling to every part of my self-examined body.

We were two pints into a conversation that present-day me would not even last a sip of beer in. It was a confessional kind of conversation where my friend, the cis person, told me how hard it was for her to understand transness because she had never been around trans people. I reminded her that I am trans in order to fight against the urge she had to abstract us. I wanted to ground us as people like me, who walk among the definitely real cisgender people. She nodded in that specific way that is dismissive in outcome but positive in intention, and began to clarify what she meant:

"But I mean, *real* trans."

She paused, I suspect to check how I felt about that sentence, and then clarified, "Obviously I get that you say you are trans, but I mean trans in the way that is more traditionally trans."

The twenty-year-old me nodded, consciously agreeing with what she was saying, though I hope a subconscious part of me knew that something did not feel right. The twenty-six-year-old me both cringes and thrills at the word "traditionally" appearing next to "trans." As if anything feels traditional about a journey into gender deviance. Unless, of course, my friend was referring to the archaic and long-standing examples of transness within historical periods—yet something tells me she was not.

There's a part of me that looks back at this moment and wishes that there and then, I had thrown the table over, broken the harmony of the previously peaceful, diversity-advertising pub, and started the first-ever fight that had happened there. That I had thrown my drink in anger and hurt as I shouted the word "traditionally" on repeat, interspersed with the names of Amanda Lepore, or Marsha P. Johnson, or Nina Arsenault—none of whom strike me as anything that the word "traditionally" would sit next to. Even if fights had happened in the pub before this one, our fight would be known as the first—as often occurs with emblems and history—and I would be the tranny who threw the first drink. Or something like that.

There was no fight, however. There was only a younger me accepting and nodding along to my friend's differentiation between whatever my version of trans is and the "traditional" one.

Although I know that no part of any of this, where "this" means trans, feels traditional—no matter what we may or may not do to our bodies—six years on, I still do understand what my friend meant. She was talking about a cisgender idea of completion, and the more recent attempts I've seen from liberal activism to categorize us more clearly as "trans" and then those who are "nonbinary." Often, to gain a feeling of progression for marginalized communities, we see an attempt to sanitize the complexity of said group—almost as if to make it more respectable for those in power to accept us. In regard to being trans, it is the attempt to make a binary of "traditional" and "untraditional" ways to relate to gender. Her "traditional" meant a gender recognizable by the state (i.e., male or female), and the "untraditional" meant those of us who are nonbinary. Her word "real" is actually doing some heavy lifting, where "real" means going from one distinguishable gender to the other, or at least looking like you are trying to do that in their eyes. My friend, in this moment, rather summed up how—as transness becomes more visible to a mainstream society—there is a specific attempt to make it less complex and more legible, and how part of this project of "legibility" by cisgender society is to delegitimize unrecognizable genders outside of the binary.

A part of me wonders if, for my friend, "real" also meant commitment.

There is surely something distinct to say about a trans experience that has to endure the incredibly transphobic medical system. "Real" could mean the trans people who have had to save, or fundraise, or wait to afford the costly and arduous medical procedures to make changes to their bodies. I'm not here to remove a way of discussing our differences, but I'm not sure that is what the word "real" meant in this case. Partly because most cisgender people are still not aware of the ever-changing, and growing, waiting list to receive medical support in the UK for trans healthcare, or the ways in which doctors are often still creating transphobic care for trans patients. But it also feels as if the dominant cisgender culture catches the trans community in an immovable predicament—whether "real" or not. Often, people try to delegitimize medical transition, misgendering trans people as either "effeminate men" or "tomboy women," and continue to campaign for reducing access to medical clinics for trans youth.[1] It seems "real" actually just becomes a word that shows that the cisgender community still holds the power to decide the terms by which they will accept the "not real" (read: trans).

1. "Transgender People Face NHS Waiting List 'Hell,'" *BBC News*, January 9, 2020; TransActual, "Trans Lives Survey 2021: Enduring the UK's Hostile Environment," https://www.transactual.org.uk/trans-lives-21; "The Danger of Letting Children Transition Gender Too Early," *Spectator*, May 13, 2019.

I'm not sure if my friend who said this, six years ago now, would even remember this moment, let alone think that this telling of it is about her. But if at this point you are reading and have remembered this fleeting moment: I want you to know that I don't repeat it in scorn. I am not detailing your use of the word "real" to distance my transness from theirs as a way to punish you.

I am not trying to position you as some unique sinner among the group of unshakable and morally perfect, angelic liberals who could also be reading this. In fact, my instinct is, instead, to thank you. To thank you for being so honest. Sometimes, when someone is so honest in their feelings (whether intentional or not), it wakes us up. Social inter-action in Britain—especially in politically switched-on communities—so often relies on politeness being the most important thing to uphold that it is not always obvi-ous what people really mean. As a result, what someone is *really* thinking often seeps through in a typically British, passive-aggressive way. Perhaps today some cisgender people may not distinguish between "real" and "not real" trans with such bluntness, but the same attitude will be seen in the subtleties of how I am treated in comparison to trans people who are binary, even more so if they are also "passing."

Such honesty from my friend felt refreshing: at least I did not need to decipher what she may have meant or how she truly felt. Sometimes I wish for the more out-and-out retro bigotry—at least then I know where I stand.

Through remembering my friend's honesty, whether it was intentional or not, I feel a permission granted to feel pain for all the other moments like this that I let slip past me. In my friend's directness, I gain a clarity about experiences that were dealt to me with greater sleight of hand. My friend's statement, "But I mean, *real* trans," in the middle of a South London pub becomes the moment a hairstylist on a job told me, unprompted, that my wig "would suit my face more if I shaved." Now when I hear, "But I mean, *real* trans," I think of the countless men who have told me, unprompted, that "if I made more effort to be convincing" then they would sleep with me.

Suddenly, it is through my friend's honesty that I sit with all the continuous ways that an intentional gender nonconformity—that is, one in which it is assumed, or the person has told others, that this is their choice—is consistently punished. Or, I should correct myself here: intentional gender nonconformity is okay if it sticks within your assigned gender at birth. We are okay with theatrical gender nonconformity, or *RuPaul's Drag Race*, or even pop culture figures like Harry Styles in a skirt—as long as that person does not claim the change to be anything other than visual. As long as it stays within the realms of clear performance. Or if it is a phase someone will eventually move on from, then society can sometimes afford it grace too. Yet if there is a permanence to it—a declaration that the gender nonconformity is intentional and refuses to go away—then there is a problem. If it is not used as the gag, punchline, or reveal but is in fact here to stay, then the façade of acceptability ruptures.

The younger me playing the witch in the school play was applauded on stage, yet I know if I had worn that outfit out on the streets I would have (and often have in fact) been punished. Halloween is often joked about as a safe time to experiment with gender nonconformity, much like the cross-dressing people do as they attend *The Rocky Horror*

*Picture Show*, because everyone participating agrees that they will be going home and taking their costumes off. As if the scariest thing we could be is not conforming to our assigned genders. Yet if that gender nonconformity sits within permanence, it creates danger. If that gender nonconformity becomes coupled with an internal confession of who we are, then the pressures of legibility, and who is considered "real" in that confession, become present.

For how can we—the nonbinary—be true if the gender binary remains upheld? One of us will have to go, and so many different types of people, structures, and systems have far more stake in the binary remaining.

I understand why there is a need to force "real" before something like trans. It makes sense that for an identity as scrutinized, dangerous, and politicized as transness, society would aim to create a binary within it. That as a cisgender world grapples with a community refusing to be hidden, they must try to reinstate their power by doing what an often colonial gender project knows how to do: divide and regulate. Much like with the original project of Western gender being used as a tool to create rules and order, here cisgender people re-enact this harm onto the current trans community: *If we cannot split you into male and female, we will split you into our idea of "real" and "not real" trans*—i.e., those they understand and those they do not.

As always, when a dominant group forces an idea of "real" and "not real," both through legislation and societal consensus, we know that it is not a consistent measure. It is always a conditional acceptance, one they can revoke at any time. "This trans person is okay because they look how I perceive a woman to look" is a fragile concept, since what society views as a successful woman (and in extension, successful femininity) is often based around proximity to whiteness, weight, ability, and conformity to gender. The upholding of the gender binary, and punishment of those outside of it, doesn't harm just nonbinary people but everyone, relying as it does on a conditional acceptance.

I believe the pressure from cisgender culture trickles down toward us, leading to a specific type of rhetoric within some sections of the trans community toward nonbinary people. If you are routinely dissected, debated, and forced to explain yourself, creating ways to distinguish yourself as respectable in comparison to others makes sense.

*Protect us, we are not like* those *ones over there.*

I see examples of this throughout my life. Growing up poor, my mother used to tell us that we were allowed to play "down the street" but not "up it." Going further up the road meant walking deeper into the project, and "down the street" led to a slightly less impoverished neighborhood. From a young age, I can remember my mother making clear differentiations between the type of poor people we were and the type others were—sticky and subtle comparisons that slipped from the tongue unintentionally, but comparisons nonetheless. Forcing a dichotomy of "real" and "not real" on something already scrutinized: being poor. Narratives in the UK around migration are saddled with the idea of "good" and "bad" too. The bad migrants are pathologized as lazy and wrong, and the good are those who work hard and overexcel—or, in the case of English histories of migration, the good migrants being those who colonize. It seems whenever outside forces are doing the work of examination, we, the examined, always aid them by doing it to ourselves as well.

Of course, *trans*—as far as I understand it—has always been an umbrella term that enables coalition. Its history as a term has always held under it many different types of those transgressing or deviating from assigned genders. Yet it does feel like recently, as a more neoliberal goal is created for tolerance or acceptance within already harmful systems—rather than liberation from said systems—the categories created within transness fall more directly under medicalization and a perception of sitting within the binary, even if that trans person's gender relationship is more complex. While the cisgender spectator was always obsessed with the trans body and what may be done to it, it seems now there is a danger we may begin to draw these lines ourselves, within our own communities.

This becomes sticky for me on multiple fronts, including the wider societal aspect and the personal. As someone who wants so desperately for us all to be liberated from the constraints of body-focused gendering, defining anything around assumptions of what people may or may not do to their bodies—rather than what we say about ourselves—feels stagnant, and not the imaginative framing I want to see my transness fall within.

Although I do think it is incredibly important to note the differences in people's experiences, what this push toward a more definable idea of transness (one where we create a harsher line between "trans" and "nonbinary") has done is create more boxes around gender to fit us within, rather than creating a tool to smash the rigidness of those boxes. It creates this myth of yet another binary, one between "binary trans" and those in a "nonbinary" category, whereas trans as a coalition holds that the idea of a binary gender in itself is less clear and fixed. Transness has the potential to hold differences under its umbrella, maintaining a solidarity for those who face expulsion and violence based around gender transgression. The dichotomy created by "real" and "not real" trans further alienates us from each other and essential-izes everyone's gender (cis or trans) to our bodies. That is a future I do not want.

Further than that, this dichotomy legitimizes the violence that is placed on gender nonconformity, particularly when that nonconformity is feminine, and even more so when it is not white. Often, victims of gender-based violence suffer not just from the instance of violence alone but addition-ally from the continual messages that the victim could have done something to stop it—and this is no different for those of us who are visibly gender nonconforming, who do not sit within male or female identification.

The notion of "real" and "not real" trans also does not take into account the lack of access someone may have to medicalization for myriad reasons. Medical access is already heavily dependent on location, funds, and varying degrees of safety and support. So many girls, theys, and boys must go through relentless fundraising to access private medi-cal treatments because our public understanding of the need for trans healthcare is so deeply lacking. Not every-one who wants to access hormones, surgeries, or other gender-affirming procedures can get them: does this mean those people are not trans until they get those procedures? Or is the desire to have them enough to legitimize those trans people? Either way, these borders and boundaries create an added scrutiny we do not need.

The focus on medicalization again highlights how this is all about cisgender people's control of *all* our bodies. We cannot win in their eyes, either becoming aliens for chang-ing our bodies or being called aliens for looking gender nonconforming. This only further deepens my belief that there is hope in us as queer and trans people refusing to submit to their scrutiny for cisgender standards—building an even stronger coalition of freaks, dismantling the gender binary even if we ourselves sit somewhere more comfortably along it.

On a more personal front, if medicalization is the way to be seen as the gender you are, and only in making that commitment will others commit to at least trying to see you, then how do I know what I really want without it? What if I am unsure of it all myself? What if I have been hovering over the same Google search about starting hormones for four years: does this mean I cannot be seen as "real" until I commit? Or perhaps more to the point, how can I be sure my thoughts about this are not impacted by my feelings of being an imposter? When so much of my experience of being trans is feeling like an imposter in my own body, how can I differentiate between that feeling and the feeling of being an imposter in my own transness? Ultimately, the question I am struck by every time I look in the mirror is this: do I want to change because of them—the myriad people who delegitimize a gender-nonconforming person— or because of *me*? And does it even matter anymore?

I can't help but wonder if these thoughts are delaying the doing: I worry that I will look back on this writing and laugh at my current self for wasting time thinking instead of acting. That the answer is obvious, and I am just prolonging it.

Yet I also can't remember the last time I read about someone in flux. Not reflecting on their transition as a past event, but instead trying to grasp the disorientating nature of being within one. So much of our life forces us into being one thing or the other. The way news or information is given to us thrives on polarity. Even navigating transness feels like we are forced to dictate it as being from A toward B, from being in one place to landing at the other. But what if to be gender nonconforming is to be in a place of constant liminality? Am I feeling pushed out of this because the world cannot hold anything that decides to expand on time, destination, and belonging?

I try to google for an answer, but even the internet fails me. So instead, I just slowly type into the search bar: "Is Travis Alabanza real trans?"

I press Enter, not really sure of what I am trying to find.


## "But I mean, *real* trans."

There are many horrible things said about me online. When you are trans, outspoken, and in public life within the UK, it is just part of the territory. Add in dressing like a kindergarten teacher on acid and it is heightened.

You tell someone unaware of this reality that you woke up to anti-trans people reposting pictures of your face on websites and receive a long essay of all the ways they are appalled and sorry. You text your fellow trans friend in public life and they reply bluntly, "But did you look good in the pics? Lol"—with the "lol" carrying both "sorry this is happening to you" and the understanding of how common this is. The "lol" in the text is kind of saying, "If we sat with every moment of violence like this, we would have no time for the laughs."

My friend's phrase, "But I mean, *real* trans," can be found in different forms on the internet. Just now, it takes the shape of Rose of Dawn—a woman's YouTube account that has more than forty thousand subscribers and a 2018 video titled "Top 5 Terrifying Trans Activists." I have been tagged in the video multiple times, and after trying to listen to my better self and ignore it, I take the bait and click. I do not know why I continue to watch things about myself that I know will be horrible, or read every last comment about me. I tell myself it is so I can prove that I am strong enough to continue despite them, or that I can turn their comments into a witty response, but as I write about being an imposter, part of me wonders if it is because I want to uncover a comment that may actually be the truth. Maybe deep down, in one of these trolling comments, is an inkling of something that feels true? Maybe they are right about me? Maybe the online bullying that is often disguised as political criticism when it comes to trans people actually has something worthy to say about me? When I type this out, I feel silly, yet I click on the video anyway. A version of self-harm I have not managed to shake.

Here I am, watching a video about "terrifying trans activists" that shows a reel of pictures of me. Not only that, the woman who posted them has the cheek to place me only at number 5. (If I'm going to be called [a] terrifying and [b] an activist, both things I am not, at least place me at a higher ranking, girl!) I bring this up not just to tell you that it exists—I am no longer interested in bringing up horror for horror's sake. It's more that I was struck by the reasons I seemed—in her eyes—terrifying. While all of the other trans people in the video were called terrifying for their views or actions, the majority of my segment was all based upon how I look.

In the video's introduction about me, the host says, "As a transsexual, one of the most important things when transitioning is to not stand out. You don't want to draw too much attention and have people thinking you're a ridiculous parody, unless, of course, your name is Travis Alabanza." The woman later says in the video, after detailing the kind of harassment I receive, "Look at how you're dressing and how you present yourself. You appear to want attention and you receive it." It feels interesting to write those quotes out. I had to take a moment to remind myself that this hurt. That there is an emotional baggage to being gender nonconforming. I had to pause and allow myself to feel that, rather than rushing straight to an analysis. To remind myself that it is okay for it to hurt. The comments in the video reminded me of being in a hair shop and trying on a wig for the first time, the saleslady telling me, "You'll want to tidy that up when you wear it for real," gesturing toward the stubble on my face. Hearing the woman on the video say "ridiculous parody" forced me to remember the time a meme using a photo of me circulated the internet thousands of times, mocking a moment I had felt beautiful, identifying the way I looked as a reason why "liberals were poisonous." Hearing "you appear to want attention and you receive it" painfully vindicates my experience of how often gender nonconformity is blamed for the violence we nonbinary people experience. Because we are seen as not enacting femininity or our genders "for real," the punishment is deemed warranted, if sad.

It is not that the other trans people in the video were any luckier than me to be called terrifying, but that there was a noticeable difference in the ways we were described. So often the narrative that is pushed upon trans people, particularly those who are more visibly gender nonconforming, is that if we just tried harder, or changed parts of ourselves, then we would not experience violence.

Of course, we know this is not true. Violence against

trans women and feminine people happens regardless of our ability to "pass"—but as I watch the YouTube video, it is striking how much extra vitriol is specifically aimed at my gender nonconformity. How gender nonconformity invites a slew of victim-blaming, as if, were you to change, the violence against you would also. Suddenly the idea of "real" and "not real" trans feels like it carries the weight of real-life consequences, beyond that of an awkward exchange in a South London pub. Suddenly, it feels like it brings with it the slew of violence we have withstood.

It may be worth adding at this point that the YouTuber herself is a trans woman. I write this here to present a part of the truth. I'm not recounting these memories from a desire to scold or shame, but because when that one phrase, "*real* trans," is brought to the surface, all of the others that have stuck to me come along as well. I bring it up to archive how often we use the tools of those oppressing us to enact further harm.

There are many parts of the video that upset me, but what I keep coming back to is the use of the word "terrifying" and then the ridiculing of my appearance. These are both words and tactics used by cisgender transphobes against our wider trans community that were weaponized by someone within my own community. In that video, all the tropes we have seen on *Jerry Springer* or in *The Times* articles, calling trans women and trans femininity things to be scared of, are enacted specifically against gender-nonconforming femininity. Although the video uses these tactics without structural power behind it, bruising still results.

Often what is projected onto those who are visibly gender nonconforming and nonbinary is that our existing and claiming transness will ruin it for those wanting (and deserving) a quieter life. Gender nonconformity and being outside of the gender binary cannot be seen as quiet: they are seen as purposefully choosing to cause trouble. To those so wanting a life of peace, others' disruption can feel like a threat to that fought-for sanctuary.

It also feels important to mention that the YouTuber is white. That is not to say that everyone who has ever mocked me in public or private is also white, but all the ones I find doing it in YouTube videos are. It makes me think about which women are denied femininity more frequently, and which can access it more easily. I first learned what it meant for someone to be misgendered not through transness but through hearing my mother (a Black, darker-skinned woman) talk about how she was treated in an all-white workplace: how her anger would be heavily masculinized, as opposed to the innocence white rage can still hold. My mother may not have been called "he," but like many Black women in the UK, her femininity was quickly coded differently, which was a tool to control her. The words surrounding her behavior in the workplace were instantly masculinized—as if womanhood is a gatekept concept that ultimately whiteness dictates.

It reminds me that all of these rigid lines around gender, the boxes drawn around male and female, and the displacement I feel from sitting outside of it cannot be separated from the goal of whiteness to categorize and force binaries onto gender. Maybe the notion of "real" and "not real" trans is also dictated by the way we are only ever shown—and therefore only ever consume—a white standard of what transitioning, and femininity, are. Whiteness has always been focused on creating dichotomies of what are "good" and "bad" ways to do something, so should I be surprised that my version of *doing* transness repels the white person, even if they, too, are trans? As if, without my transness, they would not find something else to regard as not real. Might this obsession with categorization, and gendering myself so heavily as "a third option," just be attempting to govern myself by rules made by whiteness? Trying to use labels that were written by people who have never had my best interest at heart. Suddenly, even talking about my transition as transitioning from one state to the other feels like the whitest pursuit. If I play by their rules of how I should *do* my transness, of course I will always feel a space missing, a gap that often is present when trying to abide by rules set by whiteness. I wonder if my previous instinct to separate the feelings of imposture due to race or class from those due to transness is an impossible task, when the very markers against which my (failing) gender is being judged are now a marketized vision of transness based on white and financially able modes of transitioning. The history of Black underground culture, ballroom scenes, and mainstream culture and arts has always had people who lie beyond the categories wider society puts them in. This makes me wonder if my dysphoria is only here because I have spent too long looking at certain examples and markers of transitions, and whether if I surrounded myself with more versions of those paving their own ways of being, I might not feel so trapped.

I wish I could take a step back. But everything feels too urgent to be able to zoom out, as though the voices of every mommy blog post, tweet, newspaper article, or YouTube video are stopping me from thinking for myself.

Like most things connected to violence and transness, this is complicated. I question if I'm just finding a pain in difference, but then I remember that I do believe we can mention differences without disrespect. That we can lift up our truth without denying someone else's. That transness can be a coalition for all of us. That if transness is working correctly, it is pushing for a world where anyone can express their gender in any way and not be deserving of violence. That no expression of oneself is a reason why someone may inflict harm.

It is ironic to be writing this, steeped in doubt and fear that I think are products of living in a country so deeply transphobic as Britain. It does not surprise me that in a country where, from the moment you are conscious, you are taught that stepping out of line is to be punished, transness is routinely stamped out of society. And the effects that has on our community itself are also unsurprising. Do we lose our ability to dream what transness can mean because we are too busy trying to stay alive?

I try to remind myself that when people are under pressure, we say things out of hurt. I want to hold onto that truth. Yet as I watch the video in which I am ridiculed for the way I look, supposedly like "an almost parody of femininity," I remember the trans woman who told me she was glad I existed, because "you are everything I'm too afraid to be." I look in the mirror and realize how exhausting it is to be the thing that people are afraid to be; to be a thing that holds fear. I see the lines around my eyes and wonder if the lack of sleep is caused by a buildup of years of holding myself together in public. I think about just how long I have been in flux between desperately proving I am real to others, and not giving a shit and living anyway—and how neither approach stops the unprecedented amount of violence you experience for being gender nonconforming and trans. I look at Instagram pictures of some other gender-nonconforming trans people, watch videos of them walking down the street. I wonder if they are this bothered by it all. I realize how simplistic and reductive it feels to suggest that there is this line between those who are real and those who are not, as if all people of all genders are on a moving scale, constantly able to tip the weight both toward and away from being seen as real. I wonder when my thinking toward myself and others became so simplistic, and if this is the effect of being exhausted by gender.

For those of us who are trans to talk about "real" and "not real" seems a bizarre distraction from the fact that we are all just seen as various degrees of monstrosities by the cisgender world. Why am I caught up in what type of monster I may be? Where is the person who used to fearlessly rush out into the street in broad daylight, hair laid out and heels towering above any expectation anyone could cast on me? I look back at a video of me from four years ago: I'm wearing a tight pink dress, a light base of makeup, and I'm stomping down the street. All I see in this video is the power in which I walked, the lightness not only of my makeup but also my energy. I do not look significantly different from what I would look like now if I did the exact same thing. Yet I can see a smile in my eyes. I was not worried about how others were viewing my gender: the violence I experienced then did not permeate me with doubt; I was too busy doing. The harassment was still there, but when I look at this video I can tell that I was not listening as carefully.

I wonder what has changed. It makes me wonder if this is a rite of passage. If the reason I never see older gender-nonconforming people on the streets is because we eventually get tired of being the freaks everyone looks at. If eventually we know that in order to live peacefully we must choose one or the other. Or if secretly we have a desire to finally be seen as "real." Why, six years on, am I suddenly giving weight to a sentence said to me in a pub? I can't help but wonder if there is an expiration date surrounding bold gender nonconformity in public.

If I change to become less visibly none of the above, I want it to be recorded here that I'm not sure all of it is consensual. In the battle to have consent over my body and gender choices, I want the murkiness of not knowing what is coming from myself or societal pressures to be noted. I want to say that I am unsure and for that to be okay. It is a project of marketization and its individualist empowerment narratives to make us feel that every choice we make comes from within ourselves, but nothing about my gender feels individualistic. Everything about it feels wrapped up with *you*, the person outside me. I am not sure I would be here, even writing these thoughts, thinking about changing myself and my body, if there was not such a public penalty for being gender nonconforming.

## "But I mean, *real* trans."

I am scrolling Twitter and I see an image of a central London theater that has a huge mural of Marsha P. outside of it. I smile at how beautiful she is. I wish the city was not under COVID lockdown so I could travel and look at the mural in person. I wonder if the theater has ever commissioned a Black trans writer on their stage, yet despite that wondering, I try to stare into Marsha's eyes. The mural will be taken down after LGBT+ history month ends, as is to be expected with the temporary nature of emblems.

I try not to project too much of my own story onto history, but when someone becomes an emblem, that temptation becomes harder. I wonder how Marsha would feel about becoming a face to the phrases people chant. Or her friend Sylvia Rivera, a fellow activist who is often mentioned in tandem with Marsha in a way that has almost become a copy and paste for people to shoehorn in trans history. How easily their names have come to roll off the tongue of anyone wanting to show their intention to support Black and Brown trans lives. I wonder how they would feel about how often and consistently they are called women.

I read about both in books, listen to things they have said, and I realize there are so many words Marsha and Sylvia used to describe themselves. Gay. A drag queen. A street queen. A transvestite. A woman. Of course, it is impossible to know how time would have changed their ways of describing themselves, but I can't help but think that the pressure I feel on myself to remove the less definable edges around my transness is the same desire we have to put more understandable labels on the figures who precede us. As if, in order for them to be an emblem, we must first make them man or woman. What we gain from reinstating only womanhood in figures like Marsha and Sylvia is a hope and push for more legibility in our struggle. We will take the hit of nuances we may *lose*, because then at least there is a figure who others will understand enough to make into a mural.

At first it feels harmless and not like something to correct. The thing about history, and figures from the past, is that we have no way of knowing how or who they would be in this current time. Yet as I start to see the same people who may make distinctions of "real" versus "not real" trans hold up murals and paintings of Marsha P. and Sylvia, I wonder if anyone else can hear how loudly the irony of this resounds. Marsha P. was gender nonconforming.

Marsha P. and Sylvia spoke openly and complexly about many aspects of their identity.

In reading about Marsha P. and Sylvia in archives, I found they both seemed ambivalent about the words they used to describe themselves—and were far clearer on what their gender and its expression aligned them with politically. They were too busy fighting for the right to walk down streets safely or to have sex work respected and safely practiced, too busy being involved in conversations around housing and HIV, to continually persuade or show themselves to be "real," let alone "real women." It makes me wonder if this nosedive into womanhood, and making sure we are legible within it, seems like it exists on the same side of the coin as whiteness. If being understood by the gender binary is actually just trying to be understood by whiteness. And if divesting from the first is also turning your back on the second.

At least that would help me make sense of the violence. Of course gender nonconformity and deviation from a binary would attract hurt and cause disruption if they were also a leaving-behind of white supremacy. The magnitude matches the cause.

I wonder, if Marsha were here now, if she too would be ridiculed on YouTube for how she looked. Or if she would sit in a South London bar populated by fashion marketing staff and be told that she was not "*real* trans." If she would be seen as cheapening the "*real* trans" conversation. Or if her vivacity and boldness would strike through even the densest of gatekeeping. I wonder how I would have kept ahold of my vivacity if I had lived in her era too. How do others do it, amid scrutiny from all sides?

I think of all my friends who aren't "real" trans. The one who says she is a woman in public because that's how the world views her but in private tells me she's never let go of knowing it's all a game. Or my friend who walks down the street every day in a full armor of dark body hair and tight dresses, and tells me proudly, "I have no dysphoria, I am trans." I think of all the people too busy in clubs and being in the moment to tell me about something as boring to them as their gender. I think of my gender-nonconforming trans friend who said to me, "Why do you care if they think you are real or not? Look at how beautiful we are when we let go." I remember a phone call I had with a friend who told me, "It feels like the only option is to either get work done so they believe me or give up trying." My story contradicts theirs, or their own stories sit in antithesis to someone else's, kind of feeling how it should feel among any group of people—like we are all contradicting each other in our human complexity.

## "But I mean, *real* trans."

The truth is, this is not how we instinctively look at each other. As soon as we really try to clarify what counts as real or not real, we see that the lines are as slippery as gender in the first place. That the instinct to create more binaries within gender will always cause more harm, whether that be the creation of man and woman in the first place or further binaries of "trans nonbinary" and "trans": both in their application are messy and cause erasure. As if we can ever, or should ever, tell what someone has or has not done to their body. Or as if there is a certain amount of medication that suddenly makes someone real. And as if becoming "real" stops the violence enacted by misogyny and patriarchy. Or as if all of this cannot also be taken away in an instant. All this time wasted on barriers and borders stops coalition, with us being too busy talking about which of us is real to even think about how to stop the very real violence a lot of us experience. It stops us thinking about the enemies outside our house instead of dealing with the side effects it causes within.

I keep thinking of my friend in the pub. I keep wondering what I would say to her if she said those words to me now. Or if, in truth, I'd be too tired of it all to respond. Maybe she would say it on a day when I had started to believe that division myself. Maybe I need to write down what I would reply, so then at least I can immortalize a strength that is often lost in the moment.

o

"But I mean, *real* trans—you've not had any surgeries done."

I ended up saying nothing. But if I could turn back the clocks, I wish it had gone something like this.

*We both pause. She wishes she hadn't said that. Not because she doesn't think it but because neither of us can be bothered to figure out what we really mean.*

*I look at the half-drunk pint. I put it down. I decide instead that today I will try and say what I think, even if I have not fully figured it out. I remind myself that there are so many types of people who are allowed to say things even when they are not fully sure.*

*"I wish you would not say 'real' as a qualifier before trying to split up me and my other sisters and siblings. You may think it is a natural thing to split people up, that it is already embedded within the thing itself, but that shit is done to us externally. And we are*

not superheroes, you know, eventually that stuff seeps into us. It affects how we think, how we treat other people, how we treat ourselves. Your pressure on us to make ourselves 'real,' whether you mean to or not, builds into a culture that further separates us. It makes us think that these divisions are real, because you enact the effects of them, whether they are real or not.

"I think right now, our country, this planet, are running out of oxygen. We are falling further and further to the right of where we want to be. And we think all of this dissection between us will help, but it is only a distraction. Instead of deciding which one of us is 'real' or not, can't we all decide to stop trying? We don't have to all be the same to still be real.

"You understanding something does not make it real. Understanding is not a prerequisite for us existing. I'll explain what I mean, but only if you get the next round."

## 3

## "Ladies, gentlemen, and those lucky enough to transcend gender."

I don't think it makes sense to write a book so heavily about gender, and particularly my own, and not have a chapter start with a phrase that comes from a nightclub. One spoken by a person who, for me at least, my version of the nightclub would not be here without. Someone who, if you looked up the definition of "nightclub" in a dictionary, you would see a photo of snarling back at you with a Marlboro cigarette. Although I could not leave the nightclub out of this book, it feels hard to write about the club right now. I am sitting in my house just over a year into a global pandemic that turned sweaty bars and bathrooms into glitching Zoom rooms and pixelated DJ sets. Everyone is trying to give a simulation of the nightclub a go, whether that be stage plays like my own reminiscing about it, or queer house parties emulating it, but if I cannot smell the breath of someone who has just thrown up in someone else's handbag, am I really in a nightclub?

## "Ladies, gentlemen, and those lucky enough to transcend gender."

My neck was hurting from staring up at the stage. I was seated at one of the front tables in the Royal Vauxhall Tavern, known by those who know as the RVT, looking up at the raised stage, at the shadowed figure of David Hoyle. David Hoyle, or Divine David, depending in which era you were born, was in the middle of one of his sermonic lectures about the government, poverty, and war. I had been in London long enough that I had found out that to get a front table at the RVT, you had to arrive early, but I was not so settled in that I had a reserved table or was performing on stage with David, which would be a few years on. Those who are aware of David Hoyle will know exactly the kind of sermon I am talking about, and how no words can ever really do justice to the way David controls a microphone and an audience. How it can feel like David is making everything up on the spot, until a small smile cracks after a laconically witty joke, and you realize how many cogs are turning in his brain as he performs. For those unaware of David, I give you the next paragraph break to google him, so that we can all be up to speed on who he is. On YouTube, "Divine David's Favorite Place" is a great place to start, or the interview I conducted with him for INFERNO London, if I'm being particularly biased.

I trust after that David Hoyle research break, you can imagine the scene slightly more clearly. You can imagine that at a David Hoyle show, you are not simply looking at a performer but also listening attentively to what David has to say. Whereas a lazy watcher of performance may just say "his style of drag is political," I would rather say "his form to show his politics is drag"—one most definitely feels that politics comes first at a David show. It is why I will always crane my neck at harsh angles in order to see him live.

Stumbling across his work in my bedroom on a laptop screen at sixteen years old changed the world for me. All I could read or write about breaking rules, or going against what people expect of us, David encapsulated in the opening thirty-two seconds of a performance. He reminded me that gender is often a verb. At sixteen, I was so desperately searching for people who were expressing their gender in ways beyond what I could see. Surrounded by people in uniforms, whether the ones students wear or teachers are expected to, I desperately needed a glimpse of an example of someone not in a uniform. Just to see someone who may have been given a sheet at the beginning of the school term telling them what they needed to wear, and simply decided to say, "fuck it." One of those examples was David Hoyle. And watching him live, many years later, was to witness a rule-breaker in the flesh.

I was no longer sixteen and living without any examples of rule breaking, but a twenty-year-old sitting with my own table of freaks as we received a religious sermon we could get behind, delivered at the Royal Vauxhall Tavern by David Hoyle. There was such power in seeing someone break rules and, rather than be punished for it—which sixteen-year-old me had so associated with transgression—be applauded for it; in watching David bathe in, rather than run from, the knowledge that he was going against expectations. Twisting my head to hear David Hoyle on the microphone at the RVT was not only to witness David break the rules but to see him encouraging others to do it too.

### "Ladies, gentlemen, and those lucky enough to transcend gender."

Four years later, no longer a fresh-faced London queer at the RVT, I was hearing David say this phrase while we were on tour together, at a Pride celebration in Macedonia, in eastern Europe. We met at a smoking area in the Istanbul airport before getting our flight, and after landing in Macedonia, were almost instantly taken to the stage to perform. I could fill this chapter with all the ways the sixteen-year-old me became the twenty-four-year-old performing alongside their inspiration in a country they never thought they would visit—but I find talking about the mechanics of how a dream realizes itself into flesh always does the job of taking away its magic. There is something in placing the sixteen-year-old in their room directly next to their hero on stage years later that reminds me of the magic of transition and change, something I often want to hold onto rather than explain away.

Beyond that particular magic, it is this phrase David says that has stuck with me throughout that transition in time. How David can say, with such ease, the phrase that, each of the many times I have watched him perform throughout my life, still causes me to trip or smile. Or, in the case of the Pride performance in Macedonia, causes other people to stumble.

### "Ladies, gentlemen, and those lucky enough to transcend gender."

"What does he mean, 'lucky enough to transcend'?" asked one of the audience members I'd become friendly with in Macedonia. By this point in my touring performance life, I'd been traveling across Europe with my work pretty industriously for two years, often brought to countries by the hard work and efforts of queer organizers, or occasionally by a fancy arts institution. Nine out of ten times, the former was far more fun, and the trip to Macedonia was the former type. I adored how often the queer organizing groups would attempt to book me in the same style that say, a multi-million-pound festival would, yet within three minutes of spending time with me, all the fake corporate profession-alism would drop as we realized we were both of the same cloth: a queered one. Often in these types of shows, the work would never start and stop neatly during my time on stage but would continue out into the conversations, the retelling of our lives or the excitement that other commu-nities had about me being momentarily in theirs. It almost felt more like being on a school exchange program that may or may not include me performing on stage to more than three hundred people somewhere in the middle of the trip.

Like fifteen-year-old me on a French exchange program, when I am touring, I find my usual desire for personal space—thinking a lot before I do things and not talking to many people I do not know—is swapped instantly for spontaneity, constant socializing, and intense and deep conversations with people I have met only a moment before. I can bring a generosity to each conversation, as if I am honoring the younger version of myself who knows how far outside of my imagination this touring and queer life is for me.

So when I am asked "what does he mean, lucky enough to transcend?" about David Hoyle's alternative to "ladies and gentlemen," my heart and generosity are already open in a way that is too rare when I am in the UK.

I find my inquisitive and naturally conversational dispo-sition is dampened by the gloom that comes with living in the UK, but there is nothing quite like an exchange trip, in a queer bar in Macedonia, to unlock my ability to reflect and converse.

"I felt exactly the same when I first heard him say it. Lucky? Us, lucky? But it made me think, god, we are blessed in so many ways. Like we know something other people do not."

There was a pause after I said this. At first, I thought the pause was caused by a language barrier. Then I realized it was a barrier we both had held onto at some point in our lives that prevented us from thinking of our own deviance as anything close to lucky, let alone something that could spark joy.

"So he means lucky as in we are more free?" replied the audience member after our pause.

"I mean, it's David Hoyle, no one ever fully knows what he may mean . . ."

We smiled at each other in a way that says "thank you," where the "thank you" could also be translated to "both of us will continue this conversation without the other one around," and we raised a glass to ourselves and to David, as we carried on cheering at the show. I wish I could remember the audience member's name—at least so, if I were to change it for the sake of books and publishing, I could pick one just as captivating as their aura.

Instead I will say that we were both wearing skirts daringly short, and hairy legs even more terrifyingly on show, and beards covered badly in makeup shades we had yet to perfect.

Thinking about David and his transcendental phrase is a reminder to me that so many of my best lessons—but also teachings—have happened in the club. Through my experiences of club culture, I was able to create alternative associations with parts of myself that the outside world had tampered with. I could go from the minority to the majority using just a sweaty hand stamp, passing through a half-broken basement door. In the club, the same outfit that received pushback in the street was drowned in praise and privilege. I found that in the queer clubs I occupied in London, the more deviance from gender you showed, the more drinks, line cuts, and attention you got. I learned that I could have compliments shouted at me from across the room, rather than just insults. An alternative world existed, one where exploration was met with reward rather than sanction.

Despite the medicinal qualities the club carries for me—and those definitely should not be downplayed—it still took me a long time to think of my transness and the specifics of its nonconformity as anything close to lucky.

And even when I did land at that place, it is something I certainly still have to fight to feel. Although within the club I could definitely see more people who looked like me—and representation is certainly sometimes a balm for loneliness—the fresh-faced version of myself in the clubs still did not look at my gender nonconformity as something that brought abundance rather than scarcity. In my eyes, we still had to go to clubs, exist during the night, and pay entry fees in order to feel togetherness. Gender nonconformity and transness still had to go to a basement in order to be free from violence. I'm not sure what felt lucky about that.

### "Ladies, gentlemen, and those lucky enough to transcend gender."

Although this still holds true, years on, I have more appreciation and my own understanding for why David Hoyle may place "lucky" before those of us who transcend a clear binary of male and female.

For this next lesson, as with the greatest ones I've learned in life, I will stay in the club. Yet this time, instead of David in control of the mic, there was now a fiercely overconfident, skimpily dressed, and not-yet-tired twenty-three-year-old me. By this point in my performance career, I was making just enough money from being on stage to be able to pay rent, eat food, and buy cigarettes. With the number of hours of work I was putting in, and the amount of my output, you'd think I'd have been earning far more: I blame the lack of tip culture in the UK. I was also beginning to have a small following of people who enjoyed my work. I hit ten thousand followers on Instagram around this time, which felt like a marker that a lot of people placed importance on. I do remember feeling a deep fear that this rising internet visibility might not end up feeling good: an instinct to attend to at another time. For now, I was focusing on the increase in free drink tokens.

It also meant that at this point in my career, I was able to put together tours across the UK in bars, clubs, university student unions, and small theater venues that would have about one hundred people in them (unless I was performing in the rural town of Hull; then only twenty-five people showed up and we blamed it on the weather).

Having spent two years from the age of twenty-one touring up and down the country, sometimes doing five cities in one chaotically organized week, I was meeting hundreds of people in one month. Due to the topics I covered, my own identities, and the garish outfits that acted as a natural repellent to the straight community, the rooms would often be filled with a hundred or so queers coming to hear my work. Meaning that, when a straight person identified themselves at one of my shows, you better believe I remembered them. Or in this case, him. The "him" here was named

Steve. Of course, his name was not Steve, but for anonymity purposes I will not use his actual name, and moreover I feel the name Steve captures his initial essence even better than his own name. He looked exactly how a Steve would look. His presence felt particularly Steve, and even the way he stretched out his hand to shake mine after I had just got off stage felt specifically Steve-like. He was such a Steve that when he introduced himself to me and said, "Hi, I loved your show, my name is (SOMETHING NOT STEVE)," I could have sworn I saw his mouth form the shape that "Steve."

I did not assume Steve was straight just by his energy—rather, it came as a quick disclosure every time he congratulated me on my performance.

He would say, "Travis, I just want to say that was an amazing performance—I'm straight by the way—but I enjoyed it." The disclaimer of straightness felt both like a protection for himself and maybe a warning to me.

I say "every time" because Steve came to my show several times within six months. He would stand near the side of the stage, not showing much emotion, but clapping at all the right moments and laughing at my jokes as if he was hearing them for the first time. Steve always came alone, yet not in a way that brought a particularly sad energy, more that of someone who knew that solo observation reaps better rewards. He would make sure to talk to me after the show, even if that required waiting for me to have a cigarette and chat to a line of people before him—or after one particular show, to sort out a very code-red wardrobe malfunction. Steve would wait, just to say a similar phrase about enjoying the show, remind me he was straight, and then leave. After the third or fourth time, I would say, "Hey, Steve," and we would exchange small pleasantries. I'd thank him for coming, and then he would go. Sometimes I would make the joke, "You must be bored of hearing the same jokes," and he would laugh politely, in the way a Steve would, and then leave. It was odd, but I was often too overstimulated by the ridiculous workload I was giving myself at this stage in my life to really pause at every moment that felt odd: if I had, I would have been static.

○

"Without you, Steve would never have done this," Samantha, Steve's long-term partner said, as she pointed at Steve's nails, which were painted in a coat of neon yellow. It was possibly the seventh time I had seen Steve at my show. I made my entrance onto the stage and at first noticed Steve and thought, "How lovely, he's here—" and stopped as I saw him holding hands with the woman next to him. I think at first there was even a spark of jealousy, but honestly it was more curiosity. Steve had become an interesting mystery I would talk about with friends, and here he was, no longer alone but with a partner, and one who had changed his whole outward demeanor. Instead of looking at me and the same performance he had seen six other times, he now fixated on how Samantha was receiving me. Far fewer laughs, and only clapping after she did. The ego of the performer remembers these things. "Travis, another great performance, thank y—"

Steve was interrupted by a far less shy Samantha. If clothes were not genderless and if I am allowed to be reductive to convey a clarity of scene: I would guess she was wearing the trousers in this relationship.

"So, you are the infamous Travis that Steve has been talking about?"

I had never been "the other woman" before, yet this was maybe the closest to what I imagine it feels like.

Again, the oddness of this scenario had not shocked me yet. Performing on stage six nights a week often brings strange encounters—the honesty of the stage unleashes an unfiltered version of audience members after. It is exhausting but refreshing to be a facilitator in someone's peeling.

"Steve has spoken about you nonstop. Without you, Steve would never have done this." Samantha then grabbed his fingers and showed me his nails. I paused, worn out by quite a tiring week, wondering where this situation was going to end up.

"Well, neon yellow is not my color—I can't take credit for that!" As always, a deflection with a joke was easier than sitting with something more complicated.

"No, no. You don't get it," Samantha replied, volume increasing. Steve tried to hurry the conversation along, but I believe both he and I knew this conversation would only end when Samantha had decided it would.

"Steve has wanted to paint his nails for years, and so many of our conversations in bed would be about whether he should do it, both of us not sure. The same convo over and over again, trying to weigh up all the pros and cons of doing it, then he comes to your show and . . . Bam, he goes out and does it himself! Without even consulting me!" I paused again. At this point it did not matter how much stage experience I had accrued: this was definitely an odd experience. I think Steve could tell I did not know how to respond to this, and also that Samantha had a presence that, after an hour of being on stage, would be harder to appreciate. So, he stepped in and said, "Thank you," then tried to rush off.

"Well, I'm so glad that coming to my shows has had

such an effect. Thank you for coming so many times, I really appreciate it, Steve." But he was already leaving, dragging Samantha with him. There was a feeling in the air of his having been scolded by me, even if my words and intention aimed to do the exact opposite.

That was the last time I saw Steve at one of my shows. I still sometimes search for him in the crowd—especially during my tour of *Burgerz*, which bravely crossed into less queer-specific spaces. I scan the crowds for a bright neon nail varnish, often finding it, yet the hands are attached to someone whose name is far more likely to be Skye or Ryler than Steve.

It felt like a breakup. The mixture of wishing the person was still there, yet understanding they had no doubt moved on, as they had experienced all they could experience with me. Either way, when I think of Steve—and, in particular, Samantha—talking about how my show helped them resolve a conversation they had been having for years, David Hoyle's words about "luck" and "transcending gender" suddenly fall more clearly into place.

## "Ladies, gentlemen, and those lucky enough to transcend gender."

If I had not bitten my tongue, my first response to Samantha would have been, "This is what has been your bed talk for several years? No wonder you all think the queers are sexually scandalous—anything would seem raunchy compared to that."

Of course, I did not say that. And somewhere in my

reaction came a feeling of wanting to celebrate Steve and Samantha for what was clearly a breakthrough discovery for them. But if I'm honest, what remains with me when I think of it is something less celebratory. Sometimes, when I tell this story to people, I use it as a litmus test to understand where we align in the layers of what is happening in that short interaction. When I retell it, some people jump to use it as a moment to show that "we are all humans, connected together," and as proof that "equality wins"—a response so different to the one I felt experiencing it that I wonder if the difference is due to my structuring or delivery of the story. Or if I was permanently assigned pessimistic at birth, that I cannot find the joy in this.

Yet joy and sadness can also exist together.

To be trans is to know a moment can hold many conflicting things at once.

Or that something can be seen as conflicting because of our expectations, not its essence.

My reaction to hearing Samantha telling me Steve had painted his nails after years of discussing this in bed was at first, in honesty, sadness. Sadness that something that seemed as minuscule to me as painting nails could take years of discussion or debate in a bedroom. The sadness was not a judgment—I sit here having spent similar years wondering whether or not to place estrogen in my body. I am aware of the time we lose to gender. But as with any stage of mourning, it feels important to note the sadness.

I felt joy in the potential found but sadness in how much was lost along the way: I found myself mourning Steve's lost time. My urge was to hug him and ask him what else he had been wondering if he could do, what he felt like he would lose by doing it, and how long it had taken him to realize that the gains outweighed the loss. I felt sadness in seeing how much Samantha had injected herself into the decision over whether her partner could paint his nails. It made me sad to think how normal it is for our own gender and bodies to be only partly owned by ourselves, and partly always in a deal with those around us. Even acts we may see as small deviances from expectations can leverage love away from us. It is sad how often love and acceptance are conditional on how well we can conform. How even in the smallest acts of gender nonconformity love can be lost.

Beyond Steve's and Samantha's trials, I wonder about the love we surround ourselves with, and the conditions we place upon it. Our relationships with one another sometimes rely on a version of the other person that we may not have checked they still feel is accurate. Is our journey to "own our gender" ever really our own? Or does it rely on us conditioning those around us to act and be a certain way too?

More and more, through thinking about Samantha and Steve, I realize that if the oppression from the gender binary is communal, my answer to liberating myself from it must also be communal. Liberation from binary-related gender oppression, therefore, will take all of us.

Some people, in their desire to shut down conversations around gender nonconformity, transness, and particularly nonbinary identities, have taken to saying, "Why are you making more labels for this? No one cares, just be yourself." They feel this platitude is a way of saying, "None of us actually care. It is you making this an issue." After a surge in the popularity of the gender-neutral pronoun "they," many discussions arose with a tone implying it was trans people who choose to identify outside of the binary who were causing the commotion around gender, rather than the gender binary itself and those who enforce its pressures on us.[1] Although harassment of trans people is uniformly appalling, I do note a particular shift in tone when it is directed at a public figure declaring their nonbinary identity. "Narcissistic," "attention-seeking," and "dramatic" are all words routinely thrown around when describing trans people with a public profile, particularly those who do not fit into a binary mode of transition, as if we are asking for the fuss to be made. Even though every time we try to be ourselves, there is always someone else ready to make a fuss about our choices.[2]

If many years can be spent discussing whether or not someone can temporarily paint their nails a different color, then it does not surprise me that, when we see others declare that they are opting out of "male" and "female" altogether, a rupture of sorts takes place.

It was easy for me—many years into wearing women's clothing, calling myself trans, visibly existing as gender nonconforming—to look at Steve's and Samantha's trials as elementary. I've been guilty of laughing over this story sometimes, wondering what it means about straight culture that you can spend years in your private bedroom wondering whether or not your partner is "allowed" to paint his nails. And though I do believe being able to poke fun at straight men offers a needed balm to the ways our lives are often

1. "Boy George Criticised for Claiming Pronouns Are 'Modern Form of Attention-Seeking,'" *Metro*, January 9, 2020.
2. "Declaring Your Pronouns Is Pure Narcissism," *The Times*, August 11, 2020.

halted by them, the jokes I could make about Steve's and Samantha's bedtime talk would often have a note of something much more somber beneath it.

Truly, how much time is everyone wasting upholding the binary?

If we decide to leave it, how much freer would we be? And for those of us who are trying to depart from it, how lucky are we when we choose ourselves over other people's comfort?

In thinking about Steve's and Samantha's conversation, I felt an instant gratitude for the world I had chosen for myself. Thinking about Steve and how long it took him to decide to paint his nails in contrast to how quickly and loosely decisions of aesthetics are made by people in the nightclub culture, I was maybe beginning to understand what David Hoyle meant when he called us "lucky." Instead of positioning all of our transgressions as something to justify and defend, I was seeing them as something closer to a skill. Those of us "transcending gender"—or more accurately, deciding we are outside of male and female—are *lucky* because we have decided to choose something else. To choose something else in a world where even those like Samantha, who are victims of the gender binary themselves, still have power to police our choices. We still managed to become ourselves.

Despite the barriers of the Samanthas in our own lives, or the pressures of schools, uniforms, legislations, violence, mockery, and being told that we literally do not exist—we are still here. Such a defiance and commitment to our own autonomy over other people's comfort feels like an undeniably lucky and privileged skillset to hold.

## "Ladies, gentlemen, and those lucky enough to transcend gender."

I wonder if David, in praising the category outside of "ladies and gentlemen," was doing so not to be inclusive—as banal as "inclusion" can sometimes feel—but rather to pay homage to something that can appear otherworldly in its power. Often it feels like the mainstream ways of talking about nonbinary identities are at worst mocking and at best a clumsy, patronizing attempt at inclusion. One that we have to grit our teeth and be thankful for receiving, because we are so used to the former, more overt abuse. A prolonged experience of watching people stumble over what to say when addressing a room, how to edit the he/she form at work, or whether they are still allowed to call you "man" colloquially can definitely make you feel like you are the awkward conundrum. When your existence causes all of these verbal stumbles, or long, drawn-out conversations and emails about how to address you, or badges made to ensure people can be respectful, or training sessions taken because you decided to come out at work, or whole Facebook threads trying to decide if you are real or not—it is easy to feel like existing outside the gender binary is the problem and, therefore, by extension, that you chose these things.

David's phrase simply reminds me that the issue is not with us but with the gender binary in the first place.

Rather than holding those of us who tell you we are not man or woman responsible for causing a commotion, David's phrase crystallizes my belief that we are, instead, mirrors holding a reflection to society of how broken the binary is. The awkward and clunky conversations that follow nonbinary or gender-nonconforming people around illuminate the illogical nature of the gender binary and, simultaneously, how lucky those are who desire to leave it behind. People protesting against the subway announcements changing from "ladies and gentlemen" to "hello, everyone," Steve spending years deciding to paint neon yellow on his nails, and me as a nonbinary person: all these are reactions to the same allergy—the gender binary. We are all responses to a similar root cause, yet rather than interrogate the idea of splitting millions of people into two categories that determine how they should act, appear, speak, and relate to each other, it is far easier to attack those who decide to break away from the categories. Even if, deep down, we know how lucky they are. What a gift it is to escape something that feels immovable, to leave behind something that clearly torments so many. I believe the reason I am so drawn to David's greeting is because the emphasis on "lucky" positions gender nonconformity as something aspirational rather than punishable. It is as if David sees past the smoke screen of hassle and misinformation that follows the discourse around nonbinary identities and instead speaks directly to their power. When I hear David shout "and those lucky enough to transcend gender," I think about how it feels like a pilgrimage to land outside the binary. How it is a pilgrimage that requires you to fight for your own self, advocate for your reality, and reclaim an autonomy over your body that was stripped from you at birth.

It is hard. It is tiring.

But damn, if we still exist throughout all that, then maybe that power is lucky.

To choose a life of gender nonconformity not only opens you up to the powerful community of people you may meet in the basement bars of London, but in many ways, it puts you instantly into an equally powerful relationship with yourself. I say "choose," and I understand people's contention with that word. I know that for many, it is not a word that will fit. Yet for me, "choice" is a word that crops up again and again within my own journey of gender, and it is why David's particular phrase resonates with me.

There is a version of my life where I continued to look like and accepted that I was what they told me I was: a man. Where I let others tell me I was one and did not refute it. Where I continued to wear the clothes I was given and hid the feelings I had around gender. I can see that particular life clearly because it was the one laid out for me. Some of the first times my femininity was policed on the streets of my housing project—either with a look or a shout—I recall thinking to myself, *Well, this is it, you cannot do this anymore.* Where "this" meant being myself. Where "this" meant escaping manhood. Gender nonconformity is punished in many types of people, but I felt a particular damnation that was inextricably linked to my poverty and race. Choice felt like something only rich white people could have. How could I spend so much time on something as luxurious as my gender when we were worried about how food would land on the table?

Being poor means you are so aware of the impact of your choices, you know acutely the effects of, say, choosing a portion of chips over the gas meter. That is not to say it is only poor children who build an acute awareness of the consequences of their actions, but I do think there is a particularly loud internal monologue about it when you do not grow up with wealth. In addition to my heightened awareness of the consequences of my choices, I was also struck by the absence of anyone who looked like they had made a similar choice to me. I could not see any examples of queerness, and specifically gender nonconformity, in my area or nearby—so I thought: if I were to do this, would I also disappear?

Of course, there is the argument that no matter what moment I decided to be myself, eventually all roads would have led me here. Yet I know that I have made conscious choices along my journey. Or perhaps it is more that the moment of choice, for me, has been a continuous one. Walking outside while visibly gender nonconforming can cause such disruption, violence, and danger, that every day I am making a choice to value being myself over my safety. When that choice is surrounded by so much danger, it is easy to feel the opposite of lucky. But actually, when I think of it, making that choice exudes an internal power that so many cisgender people have yet to come close to. The "lucky" in David's introduction becomes synonymous with having the power to choose yourself, despite it all. Despite how ingrained the gender binary is in every aspect of our lives—from our language to our relationships, our education, clothing, and loves—we still choose ourselves. How lucky we are to be in control. How blessed we are to defy restriction. After reflection, "lucky" even feels like too flimsy a word to describe our power.

## "Ladies, gentlemen, and those lucky enough to transcend gender."

I'm on a brief video call with a cisgender Black gay friend of mine. He has just told me I look glamorous and I nod as if to say, *What else did you expect?* I say I've just come back from the shops and he says he loves that this is the outfit I wore to the shops. I say, "It's a turtleneck, some trousers, and a heel: every cisgender woman in their mid-twenties has this outfit from Forever 21." He nods as if to say, *I can't do one of these conversations today.* We talk about other things: who he was hooking up with last night, the difference between London and non-London pavements, disagreeing about who won the latest season of *RuPaul's Drag Race UK*, and then we say goodbye. Later, he sends me a text to say: "What I was meaning to say, is I wish I could wear that to the shops. Goodnight, love you." I think about that a lot, how it is not the first time someone has placed their own desire and dreams onto my gender nonconformity, how I represent a reality they could not possibly enact in themselves. How sometimes it sounds like a text from a friend about an outfit you consider quite plain, or sometimes it's a group of cis women cornering you in a bathroom to say, "Oh my god, I wish I was as brave as you to wear this," and sometimes it's a friend asking to try on your clothes "just for a laugh" in your bedroom. None of this is a negative judgment: I feel the need to say that. In a world where trans politics have become as boring as what we can or cannot say, I am more interested in the truth that lies underneath the words. The secrecy in the desire to be me.

The truth is that in gender nonconformity—existing outside the binary of male and female, somewhere past the shame and the hurt—lies a desirability. As if we are living out the possibilities others thought they could not experience. Maybe we use words like "fabulous" and "extravagant" to mean, *I thought I had to stop doing this with gender as soon as I grew up.* It makes me think of Steve again, and just how long he took to paint his nails, and how both he and his partner credit the revelation that he could to watching me on stage time and time again. Gender nonconformity is like an energy source that allows others to find themselves in your authenticity. I believe we hold a mirror up to those who have never questioned their own conformity, highlighting what they are telling themselves, making them realize that gender—their own gender—is not as stable as the world has made them believe. We show that it is possible to create your own rules, despite what is bestowed upon you.

But if all this is true, why does "lucky" feel so exhausting? And if I can read the previous pages, and nod as if my own voice is a friend telling me their thoughts, why am I sitting here trying to decide which box to fit in?

Why do I feel pleased at the moments I walk down the street and do the opposite of transcend, instead fitting in among those on the ground?

It is because, in more ways than one, this world makes it exhausting to sit outside of any box, despite how often we may hear people saying they are "fed up with boxes." I wish we could be whatever we want to be, yet the world is not set up for this freedom.

o

My friend picks me up from a laser hair removal session in his car. He is a friend who has known me as long as I feel I have had my own voice. We are driving past streets I have known my whole life and he asks me how the session went. I talk about the physical pain, how I wish I had a higher pain threshold, and about the eastern European beautician who told me I was "doing such a great job" as my whole body winced. And then, while my friend is driving over a speed bump, I break down in tears. Sorry, that is a lie, I do not break down—more, I stop trying to hold anything in. Like a lever allowing the water to come. I later tell my therapist about this moment, and he remarks how it is rare for me to cry, and asks what brought it on. I say, "I could not continue to think: I just needed to let go."

Before the laser burns the underlying hair, I first have to scratch a razor across my skin to make sure the hair on the surface is all gone. I do my best job, yet every time, the beautician needs to go over it. She tells me my hair is "stubborn" and I nod as if my hair has a personality. While she is scraping at my skin, I think about how much pain I am about to feel, and I weigh how much pain I feel with a beard. I can't help but tell myself that one pain feels real and the other does not—but I cannot decide which one is which. I can't stop thinking about this particular poem I wrote as a teenager about being a "bearded femme fag" in a dress. If I read it out loud now it would make me cringe—in a way that all poetry you write before you are twenty-one does— but I can't help but think of the pride and power I felt in those words together. How lucky I felt to be illegible and outside of any binary of femininity or masculinity. I tell the lady who is burning my hair off that I've always dreamed of not having this stubble; it is the same line I tell a few of my friends. Yet it is not particularly true. I try and think of the moment that me with a beard and wearing a dress went from feeling like a lucky gift I had unlocked, a transcending of earth, to a damnation. I know that burning off my stubble is not synonymous with no longer being gender nonconforming, yet for me it is a symbol of a change in thought pattern—from unwavering confidence in the luckiness of my lack of conformity to being someone who needs to write a whole chapter around a phrase in order to convince myself of that truth.

I wonder what David Hoyle would say about all of this.

# The Bearded Monster

(age 19)

Three weeks no razors the monster has grown.
Let me get my shortest dress and find the busiest street.
A guy shouted something but all I can hear is my own voice:
"You fucking gorgeous bearded femmey faggot" turned up
    max volume.
Some look in disgust, others look in awe.
An urban myth, the Lockless monster out on the town.
Whispers wondering if this could possibly be real,
No one sits next to me on the bus, just in case I snap.
I won't bite unless I'm asked, but they should watch their
    back.
If only they knew how much fun this side of the street could
    be—
Maybe then they would not make it such a task.
I light a cigarette, it's tiring work being a monster,
god do they wish this bearded faggot would go up in flames.

# 4

## "This ain't a thing we do round here, son."

I am fifteen. My version of fifteen means by now I have already smoked too many cigarettes, thrown up six times on four friends' couches, and had enough sex to think I'm an expert sex advice columnist. At fifteen, my face has started to look a lot older, I feel more confident swearing, and sneaking into gay bars underage means that I am starting an accelerated process of figuring out who I am.

Also, most important to this part of my story: I have accepted I am someone who was assigned a boy at birth—a Black boy at that—but who enjoys wearing lipstick and trying on dresses. The shame that surrounded me at fourteen is disappearing. I note this because I think it is important to tell you that, at the moment I am writing of, I am fifteen, not fourteen.

Fourteen was different. At fourteen I was writing poems in my diary about trying to disappear. I was struggling with what wearing makeup and dresses meant to my morality— and mortality. I spent hours screaming into the mirror that my life was over because of my urges to replace my tracksuit with a sequined jumpsuit and gold hoop earrings. I was never brave enough to buy my own lipstick, yet spent hours fantasizing about stealing my mother's "special occasions" dark red Mac lipstick from her bedside drawer. Fourteen was a time of agony. But that was fourteen, and I am telling you now that I am fifteen.

At fifteen, I have stopped screaming into the mirror. I have bought that black jumpsuit with the first paycheck I received from the café where I work. My friends are starting to teach me the importance of eyeshadow, and what shades look best on my brown skin. I tell you this not because I want to indulge in how or where I found my confidence. That is not the theme of this chapter. The theme, or rather the problem, of this chapter, the problem I had when I was fifteen, is not self-acceptance but others' doubt.

Of course, this does not mean that self-doubt did not creep back in—my late teens were yet to come—but fifteen is a time I remember so vividly as holding little shame. Yet that did not stop others' reactions to me. So often, the fixation with gender-nonconforming people's stories is whether or not we believe in ourselves. A neoliberal hijacking of gender politics has generated commercials and media interviews with us, giving our best tips on how to "love ourselves," as if we can love ourselves out of systemic oppression. This feeling at fifteen had nothing to do with my lack of self-belief. I was fifteen: I had found at least some form of self-acceptance. Actually, self-acceptance feels too flimsy a word. Too many Instagram captions and blog posts have made the word feel like watered-down paint. At fourteen, I was wondering if I was possible; at fifteen, I knew I had to be. At fourteen, I was clinging to black-and-whites; at fifteen, I was embracing and stumbling into the richness of full, saturated color.

o

"What the fuck is that on your face?"

The shopkeeper, who has been at my local shop all my life, asks me this, in the middle of a busy store full of my community. Mothers, aunties, school friends, the girl who is always on her phone, the guy who works in the laundromat who, two years later, I will suck off in the back room.

I grew up in one of those housing projects where the corner shop is also the church, the meeting place, the babysitter, the vet, the hangout spot, and the betting shop all in one. The corner shop, in a place where the nearest grocery store is over fifteen minutes' walk, becomes a well-populated cross-section. I have not been back there in years. If I was more invested in the accuracy of this imagery than my own mental health, I would have walked back there before writing this book. I always thought I would. I imagined a cinematic homecoming when I returned to take notes on the place I spent the first eighteen years of my life. Dressed in a chic investigator's outfit, I would ignore how hard that return might feel so I could describe accurately how the bricks were more of a rusty brown than a bright orange. Or how the bus stop pole had a bit of graffiti that said "batty boy" on it that you could not miss. But unfortunately, I cannot do that. Maybe it is resentment, or fear, or something I haven't yet identified, but there are too many things blocking me from returning.

In my memory, it still looks like every other public housing you have seen. Maybe on my return I could have found the specific red within the brick, or remembered which letter was sometimes missing on the bus stop sign, or the particular mixture of smells that came through the neighboring yards. There were the essential pillars holding up the shape of our housing project: a corner shop, a chip shop, and a

square that I used to play on as a kid until I became too feminine to feel safe doing that. It took an hour to get into the
center of town on a bus that would try to run every thirty
minutes but would always be late. The project housed a
mixture of Black, South Asian, and white families in varying
degrees of poverty, and the odd family that had been prom-
ised this area would be the next up-and-coming thing, which
of course never happened. We owned our house because my
dad had bought it for us before he left. I think he fell into
the category of people who thought the area would become
something. Yet without a dad in the picture, and just Mum
working as a receptionist to support two kids, we now sat
within the poverty bracket that enclosed the place.

o

"What the fuck is that on your face?"

I remember I am fifteen now. I am embracing the richness of my colorful paint. I am real. This is my corner shop,
like it's everyone else's.

"It's lipstick. I bought it with my own money."

He says the next phrase almost without missing a beat.
Without any pause to remember he knows my mother, my
neighbor, my school friends, the girl who is always on her
phone, the guy who works in the laundromat, who two years
later I will suck off in the back room.

"This ain't a thing we do round here, son."

I have to pause, to make sure I have heard it right. I
cannot believe a man I have known for so long would say this
to me, in front of everyone. I have yet to be an age where a
man's betrayal is like the background score to my life. Status
works differently in projects, and I am working hard to try
to survive the increasing amount of heckling I receive while

waiting for the bus, and the growing rumors that I am going into town to go to gay bars. It has been working because, until this point, no adults have been involved, which means my mum does not know any of *this* is happening. "This" meaning other people's anger, not my own identity. I am not worried about my mum reacting to my queerness, more that she has enough on her plate to worry about without adding my safety to it, so I have always assured her there is no danger with a confidence I have learned to perform— one that exudes "I am absolutely in control." Secrecy, in my eyes, equals safety—and this shopkeeper saying this phrase feels anything other than secret.

"This ain't a thing we do round here, son."

What I did after he said this is not the point of this chapter. I do not want to indulge in the spectacle of my pain. I do not need to describe the fluster with which I grabbed my can of Coke and ran out of the shop. I do not need to dwell on the laughter I heard from the girl who was on the phone. I will not tell you about how the person who asked me to suck him off in the back room of the laundromat two years later told everyone about the incident. Because that is not the point of this chapter. I am not going to give you the inspirational pathway to freedom from this moment of attempted shaming. I am not going to give you the story of how the internal shame my fourteen-year-old self had carried turned into pride enough to overcome this moment at age fifteen. I am not going spill all the tea on my tips and tricks to becoming sure of my reality. Because that is not the point of this chapter. I am less invested in the narrative of my journey to personal self-confidence, and more interested in the dynamics of how we all navigate each others' shame.

I want to note that one comment, rooted in some-one else's lack of self-acceptance, and their own fragility in their gender, can work so hard to push you back into your self-loathing fourteen-year-old self. One phrase can throw you back into the world of black and white that you have tried so hard to escape. And actually, this is not about whether or not I have come to terms with who I am; it is more about whether others have come to terms with me. Moreover, I want to interrogate the very terms we are working with. Consistently living a visibly gender-nonconforming life, you have groundhog days of working past others' shame. Even more so when you are not situated in a rich or white surrounding.

"This ain't a thing we do round here, son," is the point of this chapter. Where the "thing" means not just my lipstick but all of my gender nonconformity. The "thing" is trying on that dress. The "thing" is mimicking the hand gestures of my mother. The "thing" is hanging out with all the girls—maybe wanting to be one of them. And "here" does not just mean the corner shop but all of our Blackness and our Black and working-class neighborhoods. It means the working-class public housing block that does not have any culture centers on site. It means not just my Blackness but our culture and history within it. And the "son" is a way to put me back in my place, making sure I do not move, or dream of something else.

## "This ain't a thing we do round here, son."

That would not be the only time I heard this phrase. Maybe not those exact mutterings, but the sentiments of that phrase have followed me throughout my life. The more I have tried to find authenticity in my gender, the further away it has felt from my racial and class backgrounds. I remember coming out as "nonbinary" and the first thing a family member asked was if it was something I had learned at university.

In many ways, I did not blame her, because in many ways, it was true. Although I met and encountered trans people before my brief year and a half at university, it was in university spaces that I was introduced to language that helped me feel I could speak about my feelings of gender. What did this mean about my transness? Did it mean the shopkeeper was right—that it was, in fact, not a thing I could do round *here* (my housing project), but instead something I should wait and do *there* (my university)?

I understand the impulse for the shopkeeper to discard my gender nonconformity as something you do not partake in "round here": in the present day, the way nonbinary identities are portrayed certainly looks like something only whiteness has stakes in.

If you google "nonbinary" it will look like the phrase "this ain't a thing we do round here." If you look at the images of gender-nonconforming people in UK pop culture, it will look like the phrase "this ain't a thing we do round here." If you watch TV and manage to find a small glimpse of someone trans, it will look like "this ain't a thing we do round here." If you go to the trans charities, the leading LGBT+ voices, the queer community café, the authors writing about being trans, the trans models who have sneaked onto the runways, the people asked to speak to you about being trans, the therapists, the friends, the clubs, the mood-boards, the university conferences, the panels—it will all look and sound like the phrase "this ain't a thing we do round here." "This ain't a thing we do round here" means you only get to be gender nonconforming if you are white. If you are displaying gender nonconformity, you are leaving another part of yourself. The two cannot exist together *round here.*

So if you are like me—that is, someone who is not white— but you are also like me—that is, gender nonconforming and trans—where do you go? Where are you supposed to go if you cannot be something that happens *round here*? What happens if you do not want to leave the *here* they are talking about?

You do not want to leave the chip shops. You do not want to leave the loud cackles around the shop corners.

You do not want to leave your family's cooking. Does that mean you must choose between the lipstick and the sensation of someone knotting oil into your hair? Will you never be able to do the Electric Slide in the heels you have just sneaked under your bed? Must you choose between a thing you *have to do*, and being *here*, a place you love? Is it possible to stay somewhere while also wanting to change, or do roots and transformation feel like a contradiction that cannot be solved?

At fifteen, my head felt like it held too many questions without having even a slight grasp on any answers. The phrase the shopkeeper said kept me up for many years, wondering if they were right: that in engaging in the "thing" that is gender nonconformity, I was becoming further and further distant from the "here" of my community. Yet at twenty-six, I know not only that what the shopkeeper said to me could not be further from the truth but that often phrases like this are ahistorical in their reality. That "things" like being me have been done "round here" for eons. That the contradiction of Blackness with nonbinary identities is a completely fabricated opposition and that working-class histories have gone side-by-side with those of gender nonconformity. History and its knowledge can be such a balm for ignorance: it helps ground our current questions in something that survived before us. Despite this surety, though, the feeling of displacement from someone you consider community, due to being your own authentic self, is something that is hard to shake. Even if you *know* what someone is saying is untrue, if enough people say it or think it, it can shake the solidity of historical fact.

Despite history and present reality holding multiple ways to be nonbinary, the push for nonbinary to be a legalized gender in the UK brings with it an attempt to homogenize and control what might previously have felt like a beautifully uncontrollable option. With the attempt to order the unregulated, capitalism has swooped in to try to find the most palatable version of nonbinary to sell: clothing lines that are genderless, ads plastered with the white, skinny, masculine-of-center person. The potential for expansion that nonbinary could bring becomes limited by who is allowed to be seen within it. It does not surprise me that being trans—specifically, gender nonconforming and nonbinary—has become something associated with whiteness. Since the beginning of the construct of whiteness, it has been used to take over, to erase, to colonize and pretend that it was here first.

From the moment the United States, Nigeria, the Philippines, and so many other countries were "found," whiteness started the long-told lie that whiteness and discovery must always go hand-in-hand, erasing anything that existed before. Beyond the act of whiteness believing it discovers everything, it has the hangover effect of making us all assume that everything we do is white until proven otherwise. Whiteness carries the power of neutrality.

When something is described, unless stated otherwise, we will assume, and also make sure, that it is white. Whiteness has the power to mute other things that could be disruptive, like a cloak to protect things from feeling too out of place. It means that anything we try that seems outside of what is expected can often be coded or cloaked as a "white thing." Growing up, this could be anything from eating different foods to listening to specific music or trying on dresses. All of these were drilled into me as specifically white things, yet as soon as I began to research the validity of any of those assertions, I could see that was far from the truth. I remember learning that rock 'n' roll had its roots in—and owed a debt to—Black culture, and being so infuriated I had ever believed it was a "white thing." Similarly, the revelation that the history of Black gender nonconformity was so rich felt like a theft of knowledge I should have owned. Despite history showing us that Blackness is not monolithic in its expression, it does not shift the reality of what happens when Blackness appears different from how others may assume it should: punishment.

Therefore, it does not surprise me that when the world "discovers" something all over again—in this instance, transness—we must start the cycle of assuming that it must therefore be white. Even if, in our logical minds, we know that many other people must have been doing this "new" thing, subconsciously we assume whiteness is the default of this discovery. Any error to this code causes disruption: the Black nonbinary person becomes the disruption rather than the prototype. This attitude not only rests in the output of our magazines, our movies, our teachers, our academies, our publishing, and our pop culture—but, more painfully, it seeps back into my chip shop, my friend's auntie's house, my friends around the block, and the shopkeeper who says, "This ain't a thing we do round here, son."

Whiteness will alter history, remove our resources to archive our stories, and then, when we begin to see spikes in more mainstream visibility, only then believe we exist. It does not matter if gender-nonconforming trans people like me have existed in many communities worldwide, spanning racial groups and class, because in that moment, to the shopkeeper, I am new. I am something that he has only seen the white art school kids do, or the posh hippie communities in the center of town do, so it is immediately something that cannot happen *here*.

"This ain't a thing we do round here, son," becomes a reassertion of what he thinks is the norm. It becomes a way to keep us out.

Damon Young wrote in *The Root* in 2021 that "white supremacy is a virus," and although I remember initially recoiling at this as I sat inside my house during a global pandemic, I now realize more clearly what he was evoking. Like a virus, whiteness is a thing that infects our bodies and is hard to shift; something that we have no choice or consent over whether or how it is inflicted on us; something that permeates borders, race, countries, and genders; something that will make us sick in ways we don't yet know. Viruses can sometimes cause impulsive behaviors or unpredictable symptoms, some we are conscious of and can control, and some we cannot. Just like a virus, we can infect others with whiteness if we do not cover our mouths: we can make them sick with the very same thing as we are if we do not look out for each other. Just like a virus, whiteness can kill quietly and quickly or loudly and slowly—but it most definitely kills something. Whiteness and the gender binary feel like the same virus. And both the shopkeeper and I feel like different reactions to the same sickness.

## "This ain't a thing we do round here, son."

Those words felt like a symptom of the virus—and the shopkeeper did not cover his mouth to prevent himself from spreading it. The virus had convinced him that Blackness, our housing project, our working-class area, our chip shop could never be a place where gender nonconformity could exist, that it was not something in our skillset to do. Just like whiteness had previously convinced us we could not be lawyers, actors, teachers, entrepreneurs, authors, politicians, presidents, or even deserving of freedom, gender nonconformity was yet another thing that whiteness was trying to convince us that they, and only they, owned. That gender nonconformity and trans identities were owned by dyed-blue-haired, skinny, university-educated white kids who will be grouped with the punks even if they do not wish to be. (Hey, no one said a virus doesn't harm everyone, just differently.)

Racism has the ability to halt our imaginations, and as Black gender-nonconforming people, we are outside of the realms of racism's imagination. The shopkeeper was just repeating what he had been told by his father, and his father was repeating what he had been told by you, and you were repeating what you were told by the virus—that I resembled an imaginative possibility that whiteness could not allow. Black gender-nonconforming people have been erased and stamped out in the history books that whiteness wrote, so when we appear in the flesh, in front of people's eyes, in their shops, instead of sitting with the discomfort of what new possibility we could represent to them—they stick with what they think they've always known. They put us back in our place, son.

In the history of viruses and healing, there are always people afraid of a vaccine.

The shopkeeper is possibly unique in his phrasing of it, but in my experience, unfortunately that exchange follows a pattern. I speak to so many Black nonbinary people who have had to spend time reckoning with whether one part of their identity is something that can exist around the other part of it. We split ourselves, struggling to experience ourselves in full. Racism and transphobia force us to decide what can be on show and what cannot. I am cautious about making statements about which communities harass us more, as it only feeds into a racist idea of "progression" equaling "whiteness"—but I would be lying if I said that harassment within Black spaces I once comfortably occupied did not shift and change in a specific way as I began to present as gender nonconforming.

Sure, the phrase "this ain't a thing we do round here, son" may not be uttered in these exact words each time, but "not here" is something that is frequently said or implied to me with disgust. Once, I was walking through my old neighborhood and a group of racialized boys shouted, "You must be lost!" as they intimidated me into a faster pace. Of course, men of all races harass. But I am noting this incident here to show the ways in which race and gender nonconformity interact differently. I could not shake the idea of being told I must be lost in an area I knew like the back of my hand, as if one part of myself could not exist without displacing the other.

## "This ain't a thing we do round here, son."

Those words still ring so clearly in my ears ten years on. It sounds like when the British colonized Africa, and with it tried to take their imaginations of what gender could be. It sounds like the boasting, white, Western world saying it is a progressive and liberal haven as it tells the story of Africa remaining a place where transness is not only thought not to exist but exterminated if it dares appear. The phrase sounds like queerness around gender becoming synonymous with a Western project, rather than integral to an African history as well. It sounds like my friend Shadu being kicked out of her household in Lagos as soon as she dared to wear the outfit she had always wished to, which sounds like my friend Tyreecel who sits in London still not accepting he may want to put on that lipstick because he still lives on the block, which sounds exactly like being told that something *does not happen here.*

I know it must, because I see it in my friends.

I know it must, because I see it in history books. Yet despite this, it still feels like a fight to believe it.

I wonder what would happen if we allowed our imaginations to be freed from being held hostage by racism?

If we could not only imagine the sounds we have been taught but also the noises we dare only to dream? Is there a way to imagine a *there* that is not *here*, but is bringing the shopkeeper, my auntie, my mother, and the girl always on her phone *with* me? Is there a place that allows me to dance in all the aspects that others have said are a contradiction?

If I can imagine this place, maybe it would look like the Dagaaba tribe of Ghana and Burkina Faso, who, before European regimes, determined gender through a person's energy and not their sexual anatomy. They did not look at parts you did not ask to have but spoke of vibrations that allowed them to see and feel what a person might be. They spoke of male bodies emitting female energy and vice versa, the bodies not being what the Dagaaba tribe cared about but the energy they were emitting.

An image jolts to the front of my mind, of energies transmitting through a room, zooming past me. I cannot figure out where they are coming from, but all I can feel is exactly what they want me to know about them. No bodies in the way, just everyone focusing on the things we each chooses to emit. Feminine energies, masculine energies, the mixing of both—all of them distinctly Black.

I imagine transporting from the *here* of the shop into the *there* of a place where my energy is celebrated and seen rather than contained. A place where we are listening to what someone is saying to us rather than telling them who we are. There is no uttering of this not being *a thing we do* here; rather, there's an embrace that welcomes me home.

I take a deep breath as I write this. I wonder how colonial projects have erased this history, how it is so hard to access the knowledge of Dagesha tribes within the archives.[1] I think about what force it requires to extinguish this knowledge. The fifteen-year-old who was told that it was not possible to exist because the person I am does not happen *here*, is suddenly transported instead over *there*, where maybe others like me have existed all along.

A *there* not *here* where I stand beside the Mbuti tribe before a virus can spread, where the specific gender of a

1. Shanna Collins, "The Splendor of Gender Non-conformity in Africa," *Medium*, October 10, 2017.

child is not decided on until the child can name it them-selves. Or I am over *there*, with the Dogon tribe in Mali, who worship Nommo, an ancestral spirit who is described as neither male nor female. In the Dogon tribe they describe the gender of those they worship as mystical, intersex, diving in and out of binaries. *There* and not *here*, people are worship-ing those with skin my shade and darker, *because* of their androgyny, not despite it.

Or maybe I am transported *there* to the Democratic Republic of Congo, where the Lugbara people are in the midst of a spiritual ceremony, worshiping their transgender priests, worshiping people for their ability to transgress—yet *here* I am in a shop, being told I cannot possibly exist.

Do they not know of the isangoma people of the Zulu community in South Africa, or the gender-nonconforming divinities in the Ambo tribe of southern Angola? Have they not even tried to google Kalunga, the supreme spirit? Have they not heard of all the ways we have always been both a "thing" *and* something that is "done round here"?

If this is not a thing we do around here, then how can I see so many of us? If Blackness and gender nonconformity are in contradiction, how is it that history is full of us?

I imagine that, instead of running out of the shop in a flood of tears, I run to the shop with the Hijra community in India, which has survived numerous and painful attempts at its removal and which is still, every day, showing that *this* is a *thing* they do *round here*.[2] I imagine going to the shop with them, in a collective group, and that as we walk past my auntie, my friends from school, the girl always on the phone, and the boy I will suck off in the back room two years later, the virus of white supremacy tries to harm us, but in

2. Jessica Hinchy, *Governing Gender and Sexuality in Colonial India: The Hijra c. 1850–1900* (Cambridge, UK: Cambridge University Press, 2019).

all our power, instead we just reflect their damage back to them. I imagine that as we march, I grab my friends from the clubs and bring them with me too—my sisters Malik, and Danielle, and Ebun—and we run through the streets with our skin glowing in different depths of shade, heel in heel with ancestors we know and are yet to know. In my imagining, even if the shopkeeper does say something, I cannot hear it, for there are too many other people around me to make out what he said. Or we hear, but what he is suggesting seems so farfetched to us that all we do is cackle and pay it no mind.

Or the shopkeeper goes to tell me "this ain't a thing we do round here" but then is stopped in his tracks by the living proof of us. In this imagining, I do not think of the reflecting of damage in a passive sense; I see myself and the other gender-nonconforming deities actually holding mirrors pointed at the shopkeeper. As he tries to put me in my place, he is shown his own self, his own story of how gender once—and continues to—put him in his place. Maybe the mirror shows him the pain gender can place on his body. How it told him he had to be strong, that he could not dance with his hips, that he must always stay silent until angry, that his anatomy was only important if sized correctly, that he must communicate with his fists, that he must be seen as a brute, that he must police as he is policed. As he sees us, he sees the freedom possible in deciding to choose something else. He sees what could exist if we dared to believe we are real. He sees gender-nonconforming Black people as not something to exterminate but rather something that could expand his own existence too.

In this imagination, the shop is shaking, not with fear, but with potential. We can feel everyone moving their eyes from the side, then directly to meet each other's. Our joints loosen as we let go of what we think is important and move into our bodies, where the past meets the present. Labels become as loose as our joints as we slide into versions of ourselves that transcend explanation. We realize we have been contained for too long. The shop becomes a place where we decide not to bring any more police through our doors, and not just those in uniform—we cease our policing of each other. The shopkeeper is looking into our eyes, as we look into the eyes of our neighborhood, and we wonder what the potential could be in our relationships now.

If we decide to see only the things that truly matter.

This all feels too revealing for the shopkeeper, and maybe, in turn, too revealing for me. You can never look directly into the sun. So instead, he does what we are taught to do, which is to spread fear—in his case, through the mask of a statement.

"This ain't a thing we do round here, son." Son. Son. *Son.*

Nothing like a "son" to bring me back into my place. Into the body I just cannot shake. Do I have to move further away from it so as never to be the son again?

And I think about the *son*, and how so many of us grow up with fathers playing hide-and-seek, so the wider community becomes our dads. How the shopkeeper, in one blink, could look exactly like the man who drove me to football practice because my own was too busy somewhere else. Or how *son* sounds like my neighbor sitting me down to tell me about the police and the ways they may treat me, because he felt it was the job a man should do. I wonder how *son* can feel like both a punch and a hug. Like a spit and a kiss. Like a slam to the ground and a piggyback ride around the park.

It reminds me of how, ten years later, I will see a Black friend call out a white person's racism online, detailing every inch of the way they felt pain, and my white friend's first response will be, "But you misgendered me." And the conversation will end there. For gender and pain and love to be simple, maybe you just have to be white.

That *son* reminds me that even though this statement hurt, it is impossible for me to make a villain of the man who villainized me. While I cannot stay in these sites of pain, there are some *here*s that you just cannot leave. It reminds me how I know that the next year, this same shopkeeper will give me two pounds so I can get the bus and avoid the rain. Three years later, he gives my mum free milk. I will remember the sound of *son* when I march for the lives of Black men and hear them shout "batty-man" at me in a crowd. I will know that Blackness and transness do not have the luxury to distinguish clear lines between care and fear. At least with *thing* I can point to myself, and *here* is something I can stand upon. *Son* is harder for me to look at.

*Son* feels like an open wound and conflict that I am unsure whether we, as a community, know how to heal.

How we can share a pain that only anti-Blackness can bestow on us, yet you still have enough fight in you to put me back in my place? *Son* reminds me that even if I try to run from my father, or the shopkeeper, or men—that maybe I still have a longing to be held by arms that may hurt me. I am so tired of running from *round here* because I cannot find the *there* that fits.

## "This ain't a thing we do round here, son."

I moved back to my hometown during the pandemic. As everything else was changing, I wanted to be somewhere that felt like it did not move. Of course, so many other pandemics were on display that year. The summer of 2020 saw a heightened focus on Black lives ended by police and state violence after the murder of George Floyd. Like many of these moments I have experienced in my short life, it felt hauntingly similar and also distinct at the same time. I think about the time in 2014 when I was lying down on the floor in Westfield Shopping Centre, protesting the recent murder of Eric Garner. I google the article that ran with an image of me lying down on the shopping center floor. I remember when the photos were taken, thinking to myself, *I'm glad I took off my makeup; I am not ready for the world to see me like this while protesting.* A vapid thought, maybe, on the surface, but as you lie on the floor surrounded by people in a shopping center, there are many things you try to think about to distract yourself from the possibility of arrest.

This time, I am back in my hometown of Bristol, where a statue of the English merchant, Member of Parliament, and slave-trader Edward Colston was ripped from its plinth in June 2020, a month before my return. I am afraid of the hope I am feeling. I have heard the phrases before, and seen Black squares on Instagram, they've appeared in the form of PowerPoint presentations in prior years—but tearing statues down feels like the kind of action that matches the pain. The kind of response that understands history needs to be uprooted. I, like many of my Black and racialized friends, are often exhausted when moments like this happen—because frequently the conversations stick to lists like "Ten things not to say to a Black person" rather than, say, "Ten ways to begin the dismantling of racist systems." It feels like the response to Black people being killed is to focus on the surface reactions like linguistics, never the roots that make such murders possible. A statue being torn down does not change everything, but as I saw the video of the Colston statue toppling, I cannot lie: a part of me wondered, *Is it going to be different this time? They are toppling shit over now: maybe it's our time?* Maybe, again, that was my age showing. But I do not like to label hope as naivete so quickly.

In honor of believing in hope and uprooting habits, I go to the next protest in my hometown of Bristol in a dress and makeup—with a five-o'clock shadow still showing through. It felt different than lying on the floor of Westfield Shopping Centre in a black hoodie and covering my face, or marching in Boston a summer later in gym shorts and a T-shirt. Some may think talking about clothes in the context of protesting is frivolous, but I would argue that fashion and what we adorn ourselves with when we are trans can be a protest in itself. Aesthetics can hold power: in this version of myself, marching in my hometown, the outfit represents protesting for multiple rights at once. Allowing myself to be seen while also being part of a collective. What I am wearing may seem surface-level to some, but I see it as a decision to turn up to fight for my life as my whole self. Like I said, I feel a glimmer of hope. I have just seen the photos of the Black Trans Lives Matter march organized in New York City, also in June 2020, where thousands turned up to protest and uplift the specificity of our lives. If people can arrive in such mammoth ways, I can equally be led by possibility rather than fear. If we are marching for the possibility of a new future, let it be one where I can also stand in solidarity as my full self—rather than hiding.

I have been asked to speak by the organizers of this protest. So, as we march through the city center of Bristol, I think about what I might say and how I'll feel saying it. I feel a responsibility to mention Naomi Hersi, a Black trans woman who was murdered in the UK in 2018. Or Elie, a Black trans nonbinary person who recently died. I want to say their names. I push past my anxiety over speaking because I think about what it could mean to have their names heard here. Not only in the power of honoring and remembrance, but also as a reminder that we, trans people, are here too. We march within and alongside the community. I want to both mourn publicly and call for action. I have learned from some of my favorite speakers at rallies that calls for action do not mean we have to abandon our mourning.

The nerves stay with me throughout the speech, but I manage to speak to the crowd. I speak about how it makes no sense to march and say Black Lives Matter if you do not mean us all. I hear the crowd chant Naomi's name. I let my hope mold into something that could survive a night's sleep, something like potential. As I stand with my arms by my side, hearing Black people from my hometown chant, "Black trans lives matter," I allow myself to hear the potential in the words. I turn off the cynicism wrought by my experience and let myself believe it—that in their chants, they are chanting for those like Naomi, like Elie, and like me. Like all of us. They believe we matter.

After I finish my speech and everyone applauds, the next person to speak—an older Black man—decides to wait for the applause before taking to the mic. I am busy being congratulated by my friends for my speech and then I feel the familiar sensation of knowing people are looking at me without even needing to turn around. Like eyes in the back of my head, except if they were just looking at my head it would be a luxury. I can spot the familiar look in a friend's eye—that look where they want to continue the conversation with me so I do not stop and realize that everyone is looking at me—and then their sigh when they realize I am far too familiar with this feeling not to know it is happening.

"Where is *he*, I mean *she*? Is he, I mean she, still here? Can we get him back up here? I just want to speak. I got some stuff to say."

Everyone is looking at me, and I realize the "*he*, I mean *she*," in question here is me. I feel the power I experienced delivering that speech quickly being replaced by a shyness— probably more accurately called shame—creeping back in. A park full of people looking at me, some ushering me toward the mic. I pretend not to hear and I keep my head down, praying for the moment to pass.

What the man said next is a blur. Not because it was necessarily dramatic, but more because I was so embarrassed that my memory has decided to cut a lot of it out. He misgendered me a few more times, talked about biology and facts—and made an example of me to a whole protest full of people. What he said did not really make sense, to anyone, and that seemed to make people feel like it was less harmful. Yet instead, I saw an allergic reaction to my mere presence at the march. Despite me not bringing biology, or similar talking points he mentioned, into my speech, my visible presence and mentioning of transness caused an almost compulsive response from him. No matter what the intention may have been, the impact and result were the same. He was so uncomfortable with me in this space, he needed to put me back in my place. My existence alone challenged something underneath his skin, and so he needed to put things back where, in his mind, they belonged. Any marching we had done together previously was less important than his need to put me into place.

Although what the man said may feel like a blur now,

if I closed my eyes, it would sound just like the shopkeeper's words:

"This ain't a thing we do round *here*, son."

I think of it all as a virus.

I think of the way it has stomped us out before, yet we
manage to be here, no matter what. I know and see so many
people managing to continue and survive despite this.

I wonder if it feels as exhausting to everyone in gender
nonconformity and if we are just not talking about it. How
are others managing to do it?

I look at my phone. I click on photos of the artist Mandhla
Ndubiwa. I scroll through. I am reminded through them, in
that moment, of how we have always been here.

I am reminded that vaccines tend to gather more
trust the more times they are proven to work, and without a reference point, how can we believe something else
is possible? I am reminded that throughout history, whiteness has extinguished the very things that had the potential
to free us. But through the portals of photos of the Black
gender-nonconforming trans people I follow online, I am
transported to other possibilities. I remind myself of how
intricate, loving, and rich the community of Black queer
and trans people I know is. How in being introduced to
communities of Black queer and trans people, and through
studying our history, I have learned so much about care,
resourcefulness, and love. I have seen firsthand the ability
to build worlds over *there* that don't just allow the *thing* you
do to exist but that celebrate it. I have soaked that into my
pores. Yet I also understand the complication of holding
everything in one space, how it is unsurprising this sanctuary will fall under the pressure of being a refuge from the

heaviness outside its walls. I cannot help but wonder: if I am not a thing that can safely be done round *here*, then where can I be?

I keep trying to remind myself that I cannot think my way out of these moments. That my queerness and trans-ness have always been a verb, something to *do* and hopefully *be*, not just to analyze. Yet when that *doing* is questioned and endangered so consistently, when I am told it is not something that can be done *round here*, I begin to wonder where or how it is possible to exist.

I am exhausted.

I realize again when typing this that maybe this book is a project of that exhaustion, and what exhaustion means in relation to how I feel about myself and my appearance. How can I begin to talk about my transition and my dysphoria without thinking of the trials it has survived up until this point?

I wonder if the changes I want to make to my body, my face, my appearance are not because I think the world I inhabit afterward will be free from violence—far from it—but maybe because there will at least be more chance for quiet if I change. If I am legible one way, then maybe there will be fewer incidents to stick with me. I do not think that the violence will end, but I cannot help but wonder if so many of these instances of violence happen because to be unplaceable in your gender is to cause commotion, not to know quietness. Nothing feels quiet when you are gender nonconforming.

Every day feels like a choice between the loudness of others or the loudness of your own judgment when you choose an appearance that could make for an easier day.

# "This ain't a thing we do round here, son."

The day after the protest, I wake up heavy. I feel like I am fifteen again, being told by the shopkeeper that I am not a thing to do *round here*. Where *here* means anywhere I want to call home. I will walk the circumference of my hometown's city center. I will look every person in the eye. I will carry on walking and walking and walking, until I see someone who looks like me on the streets. I will not give up until I do: an animal on a hunt that cannot come back empty-handed, lest it starve. I will look and look and look until I see someone who looks a bit like me. And when I find them, I will thank them for proving the others, and my doubts, wrong. I will thank them for choosing to be a *thing* that we *do round here.*

# 5

## "So what do you want me to call it?"

"Oh my god, I can't wait to suck your . . ." said Queer-CommuneLover.

There was a pause so sudden that if anyone was listening to us having sex in the messy housing co-op, even they would have jolted. I was afraid to address the pause. At nineteen, sex was still one of those things that, if I zoomed out too much, I would realize how scary or grotesque I sometimes found it and would have to stop instantly. Any interruption to the act and the façade of confidence surrounding me would fall. But if someone pauses after unzipping your trousers, it feels like a pause you have to acknowledge.

Was there something growing on the end of my _____? Did my _____ smell? Was there someone else from the last hookup still down there hidden in my pants?

QueerCommuneLover could maybe sense my body tensing with nerves, or perhaps my facial expression was easily readable even from that particular view. They put their hand gently on my _____ and said: "So what do you want me to call it?"

I find it hard to write about sex and not make it one of two things: unrealistically sexy or a catastrophe. Binaries are hard to shake. Yet this moment was neither sexy nor catastrophic, rather just a question I was not ready to answer.

Not because I was particularly affronted by it in the moment, nor for its surface complexity (I knew the logistics of what was being asked); more because in that very moment I would have much rather carried on with the sex.

"Does that need to be answered now?"

"No, it is not part of the requirements." We both laughed. I hadn't been much of a talker during sex before this moment.

"For now, I guess you can just call it my _____."

And so the sex continued. Despite the question's aim being to increase my comfort, I remember it making me be far more in my head than the times I had not been asked what I wanted to call my _____ while having sex. I think I had just become used to sex being a time where I switched off any connection to my body, rather than being asked how I wanted to connect with it. I often felt myself giving up agency with relation to my body during sex, yet here I was being asked to look directly at it and take ownership of it. Sex up until that point had felt like mathematics rather than poetry. The question of what I wanted to call my _____ did not fit within that equation. Sex felt fixed, and this question was about—excuse the phrasing—blowing things open.

## "So what do you want me to call it?"

Forty minutes later and I was being asked the question again, this time with our eyes at the same level as we lay in bed. It was not my first time sleeping with another trans person: there are many people who have sent me texts years after we slept together, updating me on their new names. There was one person who turned up to one of my shows and as I said, "Nice to meet you," she replied, "The estrogen must be working," because I had not recognized them. Yet this was my first time sleeping with someone who was openly trans in that moment. At nineteen, I was beginning to use that word to describe myself too, with a stumble and hint of doubt regarding whether I was "trans enough," yet still saying it. So this was my first time knowingly having two of us in the bed. The feeling oscillated between a homecoming and something very foreign—never settling in the middle.

"So what do you want me to call it?"

"Are you really still asking me this? Just call it my _____ and be done with it!"

I think the feeling I was experiencing at the time was embarrassment, yet it has taken years to admit that to myself.

"Sure. If that's your choice. But you know, you can choose anything," they replied, with a light inflection, despite the gravity of such a phrase. Not even flinching at my strong-willed defiance.

"Right, but imagine if I called it _____. You really think that is going to have the same sex appeal?"

I felt vulnerable enough still being in bed with the person who had just seen the face I make when I orgasm, let alone having this kind of conversation, which was new ground for me.

"I'm sure I'd find a way to find it sexy. I would learn. Or maybe that would not be the point; the point would be that you chose it. And that would be enough."

I stared at them with a face that said, *Are you fucking serious?*

"Okay. Well, no rush. If you want to call it _____ or _____ or even _____, just know that I asked. And know that you have a choice. And it won't affect how sexy I find you."

They said the last bit while walking to the shower, purposefully swaying their ass, a complete power move that simultaneously infuriated and invigorated me.

## "So what do you want me to call it?"

It was not the last time intimacy and sex with another trans person would leave me thinking about choice, possibility, and my future. I initially thought this chapter would be about the mechanics of sex as a gender-nonconforming person, and the hangovers that are caused by being someone who is gender nonconforming and wanting intimacy and sex with cisgender men.

I thought about the type of people I have had sex with the most, which is cisgender men, so I assumed that this would be where this chapter would start. I imagined I would start with the many examples of the ways in which sex is skewed through the lens of gender nonconformity; how desire becomes something completely different when you are gender nonconforming; and ultimately how quickly you learn that the lines between disgust and desire are incredibly blurred when interacting with cisgender men. I laid out a plan to start this chapter with a phrase like, "I liked you better without/with the skirt," spoken by countless men who have been in my bed as they created parameters for the conditions of their desire for me—often based on how well I conform to their idea of masculinity or femininity.

I thought about the man who, halfway through having sex, screamed, "Say you're a woman!" and wondered if the chapter would start there. And I thought about the man who catcalled me, then, when he realized I was not a cisgender woman, decided to film me while shouting at me. I wondered if all the men who had loved me until they saw me in makeup would take center stage for this chapter. Or whether, as I swiped through each page, I would think about those who matched with me on Tinder until they realized I was gender nonconforming. I wondered whether this chapter, like a lot of experiences in intimacy when you are visibly gender nonconforming, should start by centering my experience of rejection, danger, and hurt from cisgender men.

Yet when I think about my love life, these are not the moments that feel most important to me. Sure, these memories of men and their harm are prominent in my mind; I am positive it will be impossible for their smell not to linger on these pages and my life. I am not sure those kinds of experiences ever fully leave you. Yet that is not where I was moved to start. Cisgender men have rid me of so much of my agency in the bedroom, and I refuse to let them also be the beginning of this chapter, or its dominant theme.

It is so easy for me to think about what is lost by being outside of male and female categories, existing as specifically gender nonconforming and feminine, yet this memory with QueerCommuneLover that sprang to mind forced me to sit with all that I have gained. Not only the richness of stories I have gained through intimacy as a trans person with other trans people (believe me, the stories are always far more entertaining than with cisgender people), but what those experiences can help me bring into my life and understanding outside the bedroom. Centering my desire and sexual relationships only on cisgender men stripped me of a possibility, whereas my experiences of love and sex with other trans people have made me feel like something else is possible. That it's a place where things could start.

I had always thought much in my life had to start with cisgender men: that my safety, validity, and personhood were defined in relation to them. Like a gravitational pull of power that, even if I denounced it, I must return to. And perhaps in some ways that is the case, but they cannot own my chronology too. Just as sex can force us to jump through time—how one touch from someone can transport you to the memory of another's—I intend for this chapter to be similar in its trajectory. I'm sure the cisgender men will make an appearance in these next pages—they have a habit of showing up even when you do not want them to—but I want to start with love in its transformational capacity rather than with danger. I don't want to start with all the things taken from me by being gender nonconforming: I want to contemplate what has been granted to me instead.

As I sit within a forced COVID lockdown that has made me go without sex for the longest time since I first started having it twelve years ago, I wonder what my past lovers can teach me going forward. I list every single person I have had sex with (or those I can remember). When I was eighteen, I performed a similar task, but this time instead of marking them on their hotness, genitalia size, and the strength of their flirting, I have other intentions for my list. This time, I nickname each one something that is not their name, in honor of the many times I have lied about mine to a lot of them, and instead try and remember their gender, a lesson I learned from them, if I felt safe, or maybe even what parts of myself I hid or revealed by being with them. I realize I have enough thoughts (and people) to write a whole book, yet here I am already wrapped up in writing this one, so I try to swipe left or right on who will make it into these pages—how they exist in conflict with other lovers, or complement each other—and what they may have taught me.

## "So what do you want me to call it?"

I did not ever sleep with QueerCommuneLover again, but two years later, I'm in bed with someone who will later become my significant partner (my less-than-perfect gender-neutral term for boy/girlfriend) and I am being asked a version of that question again.

"So, is _____ what you like to call it?" asks my not-yet but soon-to-be lover, who I will later name StreetOwner on my list.

"What is it with you all asking this question?" I reply, tongue firmly in one of our cheeks.

"'You all'? Fuck off, babe, you're one of us too." By "us" StreetOwner means some form of gender deviant.

"I just find the question so awkward. It kills the mood. It feels silly," I reply, still as stubborn two years on.

"All right, well, I was just making it clear that you have the choice," they say, before stroking my _____.

This interaction was similar to many I would have with StreetOwner in the year we were together. In the way I imagine colliding comets would hit, my relationship with them was one that exploded everything I thought I knew about love and opened me up to all the things I could choose within romance. Whereas previous sexual conversations with people like BathroomGuy1 or CulturalAppropriator would make me feel like my brain was shrinking every second I was with them, with StreetOwner, I felt myself expand from being given choice.

Here I was again, with this idea of choice. This concept of someone letting me know there is another option.

Though many people assume choice is something I make boldly and easily for myself, this feeling of choice with StreetOwner was different. This was a choice offered to me rather than fought for. So why did it feel so uncomfortable?

When I wear a dress with leg and facial hair boldly showing, that choice is routinely punished, and I am encouraged not to make it again. Often, gender nonconformity and transness's relationship with choice is one of punishment and sanction, of deciding to choose ourselves whether or not others positively respond to that choice. I remember being on holiday and my experience with GymLipGuy in the hotel resort public gym. I had been with my family for too long and I was craving any form of physical attraction, so I reciprocated the cruising eyes that silently said, *Yes, let's go fuck*, in the badly air-conditioned and under-resourced gym. I went back into the changing room and I put on some lip gloss. He tapped my hand and waved his hand at my lips, as if to say, *No, none of that*. I continued to put it on: my lips were dry, and I'm a girl of pride. By the time I looked back up, GymLipGuy had walked away, and my choice for myself had left me without a sexual distraction from my increasingly bad family holiday.

Yet here I was with my lover, StreetOwner, struck by the rarity of being offered choice in relation to my body and gender, in an attempt for someone to walk closer to me rather than disappear. Here, in a love that was trans for trans (T4T), choice in stepping into my transness was being offered to deepen attraction—not limit it.

Although hindsight now offers me clarity, in the moment, when my lover asked me what I wanted to call my_____, I mocked the question defensively. As if I was still too scared that it was a trick question; afraid that if I, in fact, answered "_____" a trap door would open and my lover would fall through it, proving that my past experiences were right: love is conditional on our ability to pass as cis. I wanted to answer the question, I could feel an answer forming on my lips, but I was frozen by the foreign feeling of choice.

"You know it doesn't have to be that deep, right?" said StreetOwner.

"I know." There they were, reminding me so casually of the ways in which relationships with trans people can bring levity and lightness to things cisgender people would need to call seven therapists and both sets of grandparents to be okay with.

"I'm only pushing because I can sense there is something deeper going on here, but you can tell me to leave it, and I will."

"I know." There they were again, with that whole choice thing I was not used to, yet also the perceptiveness to know I was avoiding something in my response.

"You know you can also change it, right? It could just be your answer for the night."

"I know," I lied. I did not know. I had actually not thought of that. So much of desire in relation to cisgender men feels steeped in permanence. I wear this skirt once; you will never see me again. I let you call me a woman in the bedroom; I cannot now change my mind. You try on my skirt because you are curious; you run away in fear because you feel you cannot change your mind about wanting to do so.

Here, the casual nature of being told I could change, as if change was not only an obvious thing but an expected part of my journey—made me appreciate the potential in

T4T love. All the things that had previously felt unmovable could shift and hover in flux, as if change were the most obvious thing.

It is not that I find the question itself—what I would call my _____—particularly freeing in a personal sense. I could call it "_____" or "_____," and I would still feel the same about it. It is more what the question symbolizes as I look back on it now. It symbolizes that if I start to frame my experiences of intimacy and desire through the lens of cisgender people (in my history: men) then I will continually start from a place of desolation. Yet if I refocus my experiences of intimacy and desire through my relationships with other trans people, I am placed in an abundance of thought, with new ways to look at myself. Through my relationships with other trans people, I am given another possibility of being.

I wonder if the exhaustion I am feeling around my gender, the desire to change the specifics of being illegible as either man or woman, is because I am trying to figure out too much of this on my own. Is this a product of isolation, rather than predetermination? Being gender nonconforming and feminine sometimes feels like an impossible state, but through other trans people, I gain a reminder of the power in defying the impossible. My choices are important, but they do not need to be permanent.

### "So what do you want me to call it?"

This phrase feels like defiance to me now. In a Western society where the way the gender binary is enforced deprives you of agency, another person asking you what you want to call your _____ feels like an attempt to change paths.

Like a completely different route showing up on your GPS system. A slamming of the brakes, letting you turn around and try something else.

It feels like an acknowledgment of the first violence being birth, in which a doctor looks at you and decides who you are based on your external organs. Or in the case of some intersex children, surgically alters your body without your consent in an aim to fit within a sex-based binary.[1] This society says, "I will not let you tell me who you are. Instead *I* will tell *you*." When the phrase "So what do you want me to call it?" sits within a timeline of experiencing gender as something you are told about, instructed in, and corrected if you fail at, this question feels like an unlocking of another possibility. It feels like walking down the street with three of my other Black gender-nonconforming sisters, and as we feel everyone staring at us, we simply stare even harder into each other's eyes. Or it feels like walking into the after-party of Trans Pride and feeling everyone staring with desire rather than disgust.

As I sit in my home during a global pandemic, isolated from the real, tangible feeling of community, and also in a miserable sex drought, my memories help remind me that there is another option possible. As my mind plays over and over the questions of legibility and the pain and danger that surround those of us who are visibly gender nonconforming, these moments of intimacy help teach me lessons about what can be found between the lines. If exhaustion from the memories and present reality of existing outside of a gender binary is what weighs me down, I wonder if these

1. "'You Can't Undo Surgery': More Parents of Intersex Babies Are Rejecting Operations," *NBC News*, October 2018.

memories of intimacy can also act as an energizer. There is so much to be found outside of the boxes we are given: there is a choice.

That moment in the bedroom also makes me think of the streets. Like most of my experiences as someone read by the world as a failing man and failing woman, intimacy does not follow neat lines. It is not just in the bedroom that I am reminded of the power of T4T possibility. I am also reminded of it when we are confronted in the streets: how T4T love doesn't just open up possibilities for how we navigate our bodies in intimacy, but also how we protect ourselves when we are punished externally for not conforming. While cisgender desire can feel like it only wants to empower you in return for sex, my examples of T4T love have shown me that this radiates far beyond the walls of a bedroom.

"So what do you want me to call it?" became that same lover and me walking down a busy London street together five months later. It was the kind of relationship where I knew after our first night together—when they asked what to call my _____—that only something more explosive than us could separate us.

Someone once told me not to compare loves, yet I do not know how else to make them feel real. This was not my first time in love, yet this was the first time I was in love while out as trans. My first love had felt strong but naive, whereas this love felt like an intense fast-track course in intimacy. They were only a year older, but I felt they had lived so much more life than I had—both in their transness and their ability to articulate it—and for the first time in my life, I was experiencing the kind of love that transforms you. I do not know how to write that without cringing, yet if you have read that last sentence, it means I chose not to edit out my instincts. A good love teaches you that.

I was in my early twenties at that point and I didn't have any money, so I didn't have my current privilege of calling taxis to avoid harassment. At that age, I refused to alter my clothing choices for safety; I waltzed through every area of London in whatever short dress I wanted, paired with a small ankle boot and a bold fur coat. It was never about *if* I would be harassed, more about how dangerous it would be *when* I was harassed. It would get to me, of course it would, but at that point in my life I was not worn down by the accumulation of the harassment. I would put my headphones in, play a track with a heavy enough bass to drown out any shouts, and treat the streets as an obstacle course that I would defiantly complete. Although I would usually traipse London commutes on my own, five months after being asked my preferred word for my_____, now there were two of us walking down the streets together. StreetOwner opted for a slightly longer skirt, but a visible, thick, and heavy beard, both of our brown skins a similar tone as we marched down the streets hand-in-hand, thinking about everything other than our gender. We would think about our hopes for our future lives, often ending in me saying, "I hope one day I headline a show that is just for me." They would tell me they believed I would be able to do that one day. Or we would talk about where we were going for dinner later, often opting for a vegan Ethiopian restaurant in Dalston. In the highs of our relationship, we were always full of laughter in public, even if that laughter sat on a bed of something deeper. So much of survival when visibly trans and feminine in the streets is about shrinking, but there I experienced the joy of spreading ourselves wide on the sidewalks.

It sounds simultaneously and equally idyllic and cringeworthy. No matter where the relationship may have ended—and it did most definitely end—as I think about all the other moments I have written about before this, those of isolation, of danger, of exclusion, I can't help but look at this memory and see it through rose-tinted glasses. Ones that are tinted not because we were magically safer—believe me, one thing the world hates more than one gender-nonconforming person on the street is two of them—but because of the possibility of being together with someone and what that unlocks.

This rose tint from writing about love doesn't block out harassment. In fact, I find harassment when you are gender nonconforming is a metronome to most moments in your life, steadily punctuating it—at some times more loudly than others. Yet what love with another gender-nonconforming trans person did for me was to show me that harassment does not always have to hurt. Stares, shouts, even people filming us—all things that are frequent and common if you dare to appear to the world as a "man in a dress"—can feel so different when you are not alone. When you have begun to associate streets or Tube stations with the last time you were threatened, experiencing what it is like, on that same street or Tube station, to feel not just in control, but in love and defiant, is a powerful revelation.

o

The Tube station I am thinking of right now is Turnpike Lane, in North London. The light of the day was just starting to fade, but the colors in our outfits meant the scene was far from dull. At twenty-two, I was still trying to get a degree, which was quickly becoming my last priority as I attempted to complete it on top of a bubbling performance career and being sickeningly in love.

StreetOwner and I were due to meet up after one of the last lectures I tried to attend; I got a text from them at the beginning of the day saying "Let's go for a walk at 3:30. Look pretty," and I spent time finding my shortest skirt to show off my legs. If I told you that, at the time, I thought about how incredible it was to be in a relationship where "looking pretty" equaled "being more visibly gender noncon-forming," I would be lying: I was too busy in the doing of love to zoom out and think about anything else. Yet time is the most important ingredient to perspective. "Look pretty" would not have left the mouths of many of the lovers I've been with, who would do anything to hold onto their belief that I was a man, so feminine-coded words could not enter our conversations.

If I had received that text from StoleMyDeodorant guy, we would both have known that it was shorthand for, *Become less gender nonconforming, look more like you are trying to be a woman.* Here, "look pretty," from this other trans lover, could be a synonym for "look like yourself," but who was to know? I had no time to ask; I was preoccupied experienc-ing love outside of my body. Love outside of my body and in someone else's, hand-in-hand, somehow both clashing and complementing each other at the same time.

As I walked through a now less-daunting London with StreetOwner, I thought about a time I had been on a second date with a white cis man—who, on my list, I have called HeavilyScented. We had already slept together, and by the second date, he was opening doors and complimenting me from a Rolodex of phrases every time I took a breath. We were walking out of a bar in Shoreditch and he held my hand. I was nervous, but I thought to myself that if I found it uncomfortable, then in two minutes I could just let go. Some eyes clocked us. They looked at him and smirked at me. His hand released mine instantly, and he did not reconnect. I felt his shame imprinted on me and we did not see each other again: the only other memory I have is of how he overused perfume for both of our dates.

Yet at that moment with StreetOwner, I was experiencing what it meant to be loved boldly and unapologetically out loud—where I felt not shame but pride that this person was connected to me by the hand. Oblivious to our surroundings, fully engrossed in a compulsive love, StreetOwner and I remained hand-in-hand. Naturally, the consistent metronome of harassment does not care how preoccupied you are with love: it continues. In fact, sometimes it feels, with gender nonconformity, that the more you love yourself, the harsher the harassment may be. As if the harassment acts as a way to put you back into place. Or as if gender nonconformity is too powerful when not surrounded by shame or accompanied by an apology. It is part of the reason I roll my eyes at the way nonbinary identities have been wrapped up in messages of "loving who we are," or "believing in ourselves" as the most important solution—as if I can love myself out of harassment. As if our safety should be dependent on our ability to practice "self love." I did not have a problem with who I was until other people made it a problem.

"What the fuck is that?" I heard shouted, just a minute past Turnpike Lane station.

And instantly, I knew they were referring to my partner and me when they said "that." I did not need to turn around to confirm it; I have enough experience in knowing the tone of "that" to know who the subject of it is. My partner must have known it too, for they squeezed my hand instantly. They did not let go for a second; rather, their response was to hold on tighter. That squeeze said, *I'm here, I got this one*, and my squeeze back said, *I'm tired*. A Morse code of a sort, built, no doubt, from our own separate experiences colliding together.

As I felt the squeeze around my hand, bracing myself for what might come, I could not help but think about the polar opposite experiences of being in the company of other trans people and of cisgender people. It made me wish I could take back my mocking tone to my partner when they had asked, "So what do you want me to call it?" months prior, because I should have savored every moment of what it feels like to be asked what you want something to be called. On the darkening streets of Turnpike Lane, I was given no choice in my name—only "that." Harassment strips our ability to name ourselves in public.

The shouters continued to follow us; our eyes darted quickly down, hoping they would just go. When instead they got closer to us, I whispered under my breath, "I shouldn't have dressed up." As I got ready to turn our slow-paced walk into a run, the hand squeeze from my partner tightened.

"Actually, we aren't going anywhere."

Morse code broken, no warning, just my partner standing completely still in a sudden halt. They continued to hold my hand in a vise-like grip, as if to say, *I'll take the blame if this one goes wrong, buckle up*. As we stood there, I caught my partner's eye, and I noticed it sparkle with the same look they had after they told me they loved me. I looked into the eyes of the men advancing on us, and I saw theirs were dull, with no sense of direction.

"You look fucking hot. I'm not moving."

No Morse code needed, that was clear as day: we were not going anywhere. My lover led the movement as we turned around hand-in-hand and faced our fate. We were not moving. Two visibly gender-nonconforming trans people, pausing and facing our harassers. I felt liberated and petrified. I am sure that liberation comes with the feeling of fear.

That year in university I had watched *Tongues Untied* by Marlon Riggs, a 1989 film exploring the intimacies and connections of Black gay men. In the film, Riggs says, "Black men loving Black men is the revolutionary act." As I braced myself for the inevitable, heels lodged into the cracks of the pavement alongside my lover, I wondered how this phrase could be transposed for two racialized trans-feminine people. I thought about how love can be revolutionary and dangerous, and cause ruptures around you. As we stood there, facing the attackers hand-in-hand, I assumed this would be like the Titanic: we would both go down together.

At least if we both ended up with black eyes, maybe neither of us would feel self-conscious.

The punches did not come. Us standing rooted to the spot seemed to cause a different chain reaction. As if a moment of defiance instead of submission created a glitch in the matrix of how this situation should play out. Us standing still made the bystanders around us begin to move; onlookers were looking us directly in the eye. Moved by our stillness, they began to shout, "Oi, just leave them!" or, "You all right, these boys bothering you?" as if it was not clear before that we were certainly being bothered. We remained rooted, silent to the passersby but speaking very loudly to each other. I was convinced we were saying, *Stay still, it is working,* or *I can't wait to _____ you after this.* As we did not move, the men lost interest. Their shouts began to quieten as they saw others stand up for us. They were shamed by other people calling them out, and walked away. The others nearby looked at us with smiles as if to say (but they never do say), *Sorry that happened*, and the pace of the world slowed back down. The metronome of harassment became quieter. We were out of danger. For the time being.

As the guys walked away, we finally unclenched our hands. I couldn't tell whose palms were sweating more, but it did not matter. My then-lover StreetOwner raised a middle finger in the air and I burst out laughing as we walked down the road even more loudly than before. A situation that could have made me shrink small enough to fit between the bars of a gutter was instead making me feel like I could not be contained on the sidewalk. I felt unstoppable.

## "So what do you want me to call it?"

I'm reminded of those words by "You look fucking hot. I'm not moving." Those phrases both sound like power in defiance, yet also in togetherness, and the possibility within both. I do not mean togetherness in the flimsy, weightless way that may be put as a slogan on the bottom of a not-for-profit organization's Pride T-shirt. Here, togetherness is the sturdiest word I know. Literally, it means we are not alone.

Today, I am writing this after watching videos of citizens of Glasgow take to the streets to physically stop deportation vans, the same month as feminist organizers Sisters Uncut mobilized hundreds of people for the "Kill the Bill" protests across the country.[2] It seems obvious in theory, but

2. "Glasgow Protesters Rejoice as Men Freed after Immigration Van Standoff," *The Guardian*, May 13, 2021.

sometimes the power of togetherness in our personal lives can be forgotten: the ripples that can be created by the presence of two people who the world tries to say cannot exist, standing in the flesh together against attempts at oppression. While relationships with cisgender people can often make us feel like the only one of our kind, the power of T4T love is that we are in conversation.

Togetherness here feels unmovable, because for once gender does not feel like an internal never-ending monologue—rather, it is something that makes so much more sense in conversation with *you*. *You*, not *them*. Where the *you* means someone else who is trans, neither male nor female, and not white—and the *them* means everyone who has tried to stamp that out of you. With *you*, suddenly it feels like I have a choice in how I can do this.

Yet with this memory of togetherness, I am now too acutely aware of how alone I am right now. In a pandemic.

In isolation, in regard to my gender, when I am trying to explain my gender to a doctor, in order to convince them I have always needed something I am not sure I need: I am alone. When I am reading tweets dissecting our existence: I am alone. When I am walking across to the shops to get my pack of cigarettes: I am alone. Maybe the exhaustion is not inherent in existing as gender nonconforming and trans but rather a reminder that to be in togetherness gives you more options. Maybe if I am not alone, I could do this.

I open up Instagram. I scroll and see many different profiles. I see the accounts of gender-nonconforming artists Alok and Basit. I see the profiles of two ex-lovers, who are now visibly gender nonconforming, and then I see a photograph of a group of Black gender-nonconforming people. I click on a video of a person called Afi. I do not know how they identify, if they use the word "trans" or not, but I see them Black and in a dress and twirling and walking and none of it matters. I see them standing boldly in their own self. Adorned in their power. I ignore what I know about Instagram pictures often being a façade for reality, and instead hope there is some truth within the pixels. I feel power, and it is not a form of self-empowerment but a power that directly comes from being with other people. I feel a sense of being able to forge my own path, as if illegibility feels better when it is with them. When I am in dialogue with other people's genders, I know that I have a choice about my own. I look at their photos and I think if they could speak they would be asking, *So what do you want to call it?* Where the *it* also means my gender and its expression. Where the *it* means I can do this however I want, come and join us.

In my mind, the binary of sexual and nonsexual intimacy no longer makes sense. Instead, I see the intimacy of a lover, or me and my girls walking down the street, or staring at your Instagram picture, or a friend deciding to dance with me at the club, all as possible intimacies that may just keep me alive. I wonder if all this exhaustion I am feeling around my gender and its possibility is because isolation has turned my gender into a solo project rather than a communal one. To be boldly gender nonconforming and in public is to say, *I can only do this if you do it too; what if we take the risk together?*

I think back to the moment my then-lover StreetOwner turned around and held my hand as the men approached us. As we stood there, heels digging into the concrete, it felt like we were standing for something other than ourselves. As if with the hand squeeze, they were not only saying, *I got you*, but also whispering, *Some things are worth standing for.* As the men who were shouting at us walked toward us,

I knew that in that moment, staying ourselves and staying together were more important than our immediate safety. In making that choice, together, we decided that a black eye was worth refusing to lower our heads—that if we were to go out, at least we would go out as ourselves.

I often think about disappearances and gender nonconformity. Partly in terms of my body—as I grow older, I worry I will become tired of being so visibly disruptive in my gender that I shall cease to be so, and that there will be no archive that I once stood here as I am now. That the world will forget I was once as I am now, and that I withstood so much in this form. Yet I also worry about disappearance in the literal sense. As a man is following me, I worry that he could just pick me up and take me away, and that no one would know. Or that he could carry me away in broad daylight and no one would stop him. It might sound dramatic, but I am no longer surprised by the inaction of others on the streets to protect us. There was something in the moment both my partner and I pressed our heels firmly into the ground that said: *This feels too real to disappear.* If I am in connection with another one of us, how can they say we were not here?

Yet, of course, if your love is constantly surrounded by moments of having to dig heels into pavement just to survive, eventually your legs will get tired. In my life, whenever I have felt weak, cisgender men have often seemed alluring to me— as if they can promise a stability that I cannot obtain from my own gender or, in this case, a stability and protection I could not find in StreetOwner's love too.

o

"So what do you want me to call it?" says FemLover.

"Um, I guess just cross-dressing, then," I reply. It is clear I am no longer in bed with StreetOwner or QueerCommuneLover. On paper, it sounds like the same question that those lovers asked, yet in reality the worlds could not feel further apart.

Out of the bed of my soon-to-be-no-longer lover, I'm taking advantage of our open relationship in the bedroom of a man called FemLover who I met on Grindr. Exhausted by the labor and complications of what happens when the poetic love of T4T sex goes wrong, all I was after was mechanical sex that would not involve the vulnerability of fully showing up for someone else. I turn up and take off my clothes and like clockwork, all the past memories of sex with men flood the room. He says to only "show my ass." I assume that seeing my _____ would make him question too much. I oblige. I am not sure why; I guess I want to see if I can still do this. To see if I can still be with someone who is not one of *us*. I carry on, and he feels up my leg, and his hand moves back sharply. I flinch. He was not threatening; my reaction was just a force of habit.

"You don't shave your legs?" says FemLover.

I can't believe I am here. I have gone from what felt like so much choice, to so little. "I thought you were transgendering the other way."

It feels like I've stepped away from possibilities and into limitations, away from a love that does not reduce my gender to my parts, and in turn my worth, and onto the tightrope that is being in relation to cisgender men.

"So what do you want to call it?"

I am tired. I comply. I choose a form of ease over myself. "Um, I guess just cross-dressing then."

I am not shaming myself for my choice, yet as I write

this, I have to laugh at the part of me that once believed the lies cisgender media has often fed me about trans-feminine transitions. So often I have found that people frame our embodiment of femininity as a fetish to be seen as attractive by straight men, to be seen as successful only when we are in relation with them. Anti-trans commentators online often denote our expression of gender as a kink of wanting to be with cisgender men. This could not be further from my desires. I wish my gender expression could not be seen by any of them, that it magically transitioned into a trans invisibility—where cisgender men could never interact with me ever again. Sure, I'd lose some good ones along the way, but if none of them ever saw me again, that would make it all worth it.

The truth is that experiences like the one with FemLover from Grindr still do feel like a rejection. Not rejection in the traditional sense—we still had sex—but rejection as a reminder that to be gender nonconforming is to have others reject parts of you in order to feel okay desiring you. FemLover could be so many other men who have chosen their comfort over my fullness. It is like NiceCar guy, who would pick me up from my house when I was sixteen and drive me to his. We would have sex and then he would drive me home. One time, he was driving past me and saw me in a skirt and Doc Martens, and then sent me a text saying never to see him ever again. He said, "I don't do shit like that."

It is not just cis straight men who are affected by my transition into embodying the fullness of my gender-nonconforming trans femininity. The queer men who used to hit on me in clubs, on dating apps, or at parties now only want my number to ask me questions about diversity and inclusion. They put our femininity on podiums in clubs, tell us to "werk" and that we are "fierce," but they do not desire us. They want proximity to us so they can borrow our clothing for the nightclub, play out their fantasies using the energy of our bravery, but they do not want to hold hands with us in the street. While sex with the "straight" cisgender man feels like shrinking my possibilities through how he relates to me, the queer cisgender man avoids intimacy with me because he is afraid of what possibility I could bring him. Sure, the trend of advertising for masc4masc may no longer be as prominent among socially-conscious queer cis men, but where gender-nonconforming trans people are placed in both queer and straight society remains conditional. It is dependent on how well we perform a specific part of gender. Being in flux, a liminal space, is not possible; the love and desire for us are provisional.

## "So what do you want to call it?"

It is my turn now to ask the question. No longer talking about what to name our _____ but instead asking StreetOwner to choose their own words for their clearly deteriorating mental health.

"I guess, depression? Or exhaustion? I'm not sure."

"Do you want to end our relationship?"

"I don't want to. But I can't sort myself out, let alone each other."

A year and a half after my then-lover asked me what I wanted to call my _____, we were in a cycle of trying to break up. I had done break-ups before and would have more of them after this moment: they all hurt in different ways, but this one felt particularly tricky. Everything around it felt explosive, even if in the center, it was calm. We used words like "tired," or "exhausted," or "sad," worried we would hurt each other.

Looking at it now, I see two people trying to maintain stability in a world that wanted to deprive them of it. It sounds grand, and I want to resist the urge to politically analyze something that is as intimately human as love—but distance has made me wonder, if we met now, what would be different. Or to be specific: how much the pace of life that comes with being Brown, visibly gender nonconforming, and worried about money makes maintaining love together an extremely uphill battle.

In my theory, a T4T love between two transfeminine gender-nonconforming people unlocks possibility, but in my reality I also found that it left us swimming upstream ridiculously hard. *Harassment* could be the only word written on this page and it still would not reflect how much it consumes your day when you present as we did. Let alone presenting as that together. And how is it possible for that not to seep off the streets and into your bedroom?

What happens when you do not feel like superheroes digging heels into pavement and instead want to lower your head and have a quiet day? Or what if one of you wants to hide and the other wants to take up space?

In the same way the presence of others like me can alleviate internal gender wars, what if in the same breath it exacerbates them? What if your transition begins to map onto someone else's exactly at the point where your dysphoria bursts, and each choice around your gender becomes hard to distinguish as yours or theirs?

Togetherness is powerful, but it also requires so much work. And when the world is under-resourcing you and your community in so many ways, where is the time to do this work?

If we are both fighting off danger in the streets, queueing for years for the doctor to give us one appointment, muting articles online that tell us we are not real, convincing our workplaces to allow us to change our pronouns on the work computers, telling our family members to use our right pronouns, engaging in troubling conversations every week, fending off the transphobia inherent in cis queer spaces— then what does that leave for each other?[3]

I am oversimplifying it: I know it is possible, but it is also impossible not to mention the weight that begins to press down on our relationships. I cannot help but think that if the world made it easier for us to exist in a liminal space within gender, then there are so many aspects of our lives that could be more sustainable—including love. I wonder whether, if the world made trans people's lives easier to inhabit, our love would feel less exhausting to try and survive.

Yet that is not the reality—and StreetOwner became a love about whom I had to wonder "what if?" What if we had been supported? What if we had been allowed to be?


## "So what do you want to call it?"

I've started dating again, and my friend is asking me about my most recent date with a man.

"I'm not sure, I guess like, secondhand privilege?" We both laugh. The date was with a Black man who is six foot

3. "A Look at Transphobia within the LGBTQ Community," *Victory Institute*, August 9, 2018.

four. On my list, this guy is called HollowCharmer, in the sense that he had all the right words, without any pulse and energy behind them. Like an incredible script delivered by an actor who only got the part yesterday. All the words felt right, yet the heart and soul of it were missing. Unlike StreetOwner or QueerCommuneLover, who, no matter what interaction, had heart and soul in abundance. Something that maybe trans people have in swathes, and cisgender men must rehearse to have?

HollowCharmer took me to a restaurant—I think it was the last date I went on before the world shut down. He told me to "dress up" for the date, and I had to follow my instincts and interpret that with my own choices, rather than what he may have wanted. I wore a black dress and tights and an all-black heel; I styled my hair in loose curls. I avoided putting on colorful glasses: I wanted him to think I could still do "classic." As if there is anything *classic* about me.

Clearly, "dress up" was on my mind.

The date was actually really nice. We spoke about everything other than gender, laughed about memes we had seen, and bonded over a shared love of jazz music. He said next time he'd take me to a jazz club he knew, and I pretended that I hadn't been taken there on a date before. I lied to him and said I was getting a Tube home because I wanted to seem down to earth, so he insisted on walking me to the station. I was nervous; I didn't know if I would be stared at, and I knew that a confident and charming cisgender man can crumble at the first sight of transphobic judgment. I downed a tequila shot and walked outside in the busy streets of Shoreditch with him—a place where, despite people's belief that hipster spots do not contain bigotry, I had been harassed multiple times. I walked outside and he took my hand—no Morse code between us, but something was there. And I braced myself for what was to come, as I could tell he was oblivious to anything other than romance. And then . . .

Nothing.

Really. We just walked down the street. I could sense some people darting their eyes to me, and then seeing him, and nodding.

Was this protection? Was I imagining this? Was I safer because of him? Was this a trade-off I wanted to make?

I tried to squeeze his hand when a guy nodded to him, as if to say, *Wow, that guy wanted to shout at me, but then your version of masculinity trumped his so I think his urge to shout turned to respect, for you—and then in relation to that, protection for me*—but he did not squeeze back.

In that moment, I definitely missed the magic of Morse code.

I thought about StreetOwner; of what could have been; of choice. And wondered if HollowCharmer would later ask me what I want to call my _____.

# 6

## "Children sacrificed to appease trans lobby."

I wake up to what sounds like an alarm buzzing on the glass of my bedside table in Manchester. I thought I had turned it off. It is the morning of the press performance for the show *Jubilee*, in which I have my first major lead theater role, and it's my chance to sleep late after a strenuous few months of rehearsals. My phone keeps buzzing. It really must be my alarm: it carries all the ferocity and consistency of an iPhone alarm against a hard surface. I reach over to grab it, sleepily press the place I have etched into my mind as the snooze button on the screen, yet the buzzing continues. I press all the possible buttons on the screen, not taking aim, but hoping one finger will stop the intrusive and unwelcome wake-up call. The vibrating just gets louder, with syncopated rhythms now as the buzzing increases. Is my phone broken? Why won't it just shut the fuck up?

I put on my glasses—the vibrating now feels like the phone is about to detonate at any moment—and I look at the shaking screen, which seems to be at max capacity.

The notification center is updating so quickly that it is falling over itself, and it dawns on me that this is not an issue with an alarm.

I look at the phone. The time is 11:30 a.m.; I must have

actually slept in. The screen continues moving at a rapid pace. The notifications screen summarizes the chaos that has ensued:

99+ Twitter notifications
72 missed calls
423 emails

And a text at the top of the screen from my partner at the time, which reads:

"I have just seen the articles about Topshop and the changing rooms, are you okay?"

As the phone vibrates, I struggle to get through the lock screen as my iPhone's pace weakens due to the volume of attention it is receiving. I feel my hand detach from the phone and my body leave my bedroom as I completely zoom out of reality.

## "Children sacrificed to appease trans lobby."

These words were written by Janice Turner in *The Times*, November 11, 2017.

There is this thing I have been guilty of doing through-out the last ten years of experiencing violence based around my gender nonconformity. It is a thing my friends notice, my therapist notices, and I notice too. In the course of read-ing this book, you might have as well: I call it "zooming out." When something happens, instead of looking the thing straight in the eyes, I speedily transport myself above the ground to view the situation from above. With distance,

I can dissect it, analyze it, comment on its impact on the surrounding areas, link it to previous historical moments, and discuss how it is affecting those around the situation—all without ever looking it in the eye. Avoidance or coping—maybe the two are not so different.

Using the phrase "zooming out" is a softer way of saying: leaving my body. Which is a less medical way of saying: dissociating. You can use the word "zoom" as many times as you wish in one day and no one will stop to ask you if you are okay, the conversation will not halt awkwardly, and ultimately you do not have to reckon with how often you are leaving the ground to float past the realities of violence. I think in some ways, this book is a dance between the part of me that wants to write toward myself and the part of me who is too scared to do so, and must zoom out in order to feel like I can face it. Sometimes the dance feels useful; other times it feels completely off-rhythm.

When I first wrote this chapter, I had to delete most of it after giving it to a friend. They replied to me saying, "This was one of the most traumatic experiences of your life and when I am reading it, I cannot feel anything: you have listed all these moments just to get to the analysis."

I wanted to reply, "Thank you so much, mission accomplished."

Yet I stopped at "Thank you," because I knew in reality this friend was doing what so many of my fellow gender-nonconforming trans friends have done throughout my life—allowing me to step toward a closer version of myself.

I said to the friend, "It is hard to write about a moment that, as soon as I saw it coming, I zoomed out in order *not* to experience it. I am not sure if I ever zoomed back in. Maybe

I wrote it out like a list because I had to read about what had happened afterward—in articles, text messages, Facebook statuses—because I had already zoomed out too far to really experience it for myself."

By zooming out, going somewhere far above something as contentious and unreliable as my body, I am able to make a report about what happened. Putting enough distance between the moment, myself, and the ground to talk without showing how scared I was, and am. Zooming out far enough that if the gravitas of the moment washes over something as small as one single person, it will just be my empty body that floats away without me consciously there. I become a passive observer to the violence washing over me. If you were to read my report, it would be as follows:

*A week in November 2017*
On the day of the incident, Travis entered a Topshop in Manchester to buy a dress for the press night of a show. Looking visibly gender nonconforming, they knew the male changing rooms would be an unsafe place to change and walked instead into the Topshop women's changing rooms.

They were asked to leave, being told they "made the other customers feel uncomfortable." Rudely and abruptly. As if they were doing something wrong.

They tweeted about the incident, telling Topshop how this made them feel. They went to bed.

They woke up to thousands of notifications, newspaper articles, texts, and calls. The headlines were saying Travis's tweet had changed Topshop's policy to gender-neutral changing rooms, but the assertion that Travis's tweet was the trigger for policy change was debunked elsewhere.[1]

As this occurred during a growing media campaign against trans people, the British media used this moment as newspaper content. Countless articles were written about Travis; they received thousands of death threats that week; people protested about them in the street; their address was leaked online; and the theater that had hired Travis was even told to fire them. They carried on performing in the show. The positive reviews could not be seen under the number of transphobic articles about Topshop.

A week after the incident, just as the online culture was moving to a different part of the war, an article that would become part of the award-winning journalist Janice Turner's resume was published in *The Times*. In the article, Janice Turner suggests that companies trying to create more gender-neutral spaces would do so to the detriment of children's safety. The article was titled "Children sacrificed to appease trans lobby."

I do not know how to write about something that both changed and confirmed my life at the same time.

Changed, in the sense that I had never before experienced what it means to be spoken about in the news, on the streets, on television, on blogs, and in articles all at the same time. I had never before experienced the feeling of waking up and believing that at any given moment you may explode

1. "Topshop Abolishes Women-Only Fitting Rooms and Makes ALL of Them Unisex," *Sun*, November 8, 2017; "Topshop Removes Women-Only Changing Rooms," *Independent*, November 8, 2017.

due to a pressure whose origin you cannot pinpoint. I do not know how to write about how it feels having to tell my mother I am okay, as her friends ask her at work if she has seen the news. What it means to see old photos of myself dredged up to be ridiculed online by trolls who label themselves "feminist"—circling photos of my bulge, highlighting my beard, and calling me a danger to society. I do not know how to write about how, eventually, when there are thousands of people telling you that you are a monster, you may come to believe it.

I do not know how to write about it, yet in some ways I already have. In many ways it confirmed what I already knew about my life on a smaller scale. I had already had a chicken burger thrown at me, had people looking at me in the street, strangers forming opinions about me, family gossiping about me, people thinking I am a danger to society—just because I look like someone the world labels a "man in a dress." Okay, before, it had not been broadcast so widely that it landed on the trending topics list on Twitter, yet this moment confirmed the sad reality of what I already knew: being trans is dangerous. Being visibly gender nonconforming is dangerous. Being Black is dangerous. You may not know what shape that danger will take: it may take the form of a phone vibrating for seven hours straight, or a whisper in the street, or a news presenter mocking your appearance on national television, but you know the danger will arrive nevertheless.

And as I read the newspaper article equating my entering a changing room to the sacrifice of children, I left my body—as if I had done this dance before—practicing a protective measure I have learned over time, ready for when all eyes are about to be on me.

# "Children sacrificed to appease trans lobby."

I have not read the article by Janice Turner since November 2017. It has been referenced in many dissertations by queer and trans scholars studying the rise of anti-trans media in the UK. I read their analysis, almost forgetting that I was the subject of the very article being dissected. I still could not read it again. It was almost as if it had become too much of an emblem for me to feel ownership of it. My hands would shake when I saw it, or as my eyes looked at the words, all I would see were the many other think-pieces, articles, texts, and tweets that had been written in response. However, for the purposes of this chapter, I felt it would be silly not to try and read it. To attempt to place my feet back on the ground.

## "Children sacrificed to appease trans lobby."

I close the laptop again.

I cannot get past the title. I realize it is the title that stops me from rereading it; every word of the headline hits me with a snarling bite. When I see the specific placement of the words next to each other, it makes my mouth dry up, my Adam's apple harden, and the hair on my legs curl. I notice every part of my body that they ridicule.

## "Children sacrificed to appease trans lobby."

I carry on reading. I will not zoom out. I want to be here and present to read these words. I move past the title, resisting the urge to close the laptop screen again.

The opening paragraph reads:

Travis Alabanza is a performance artist who, in the
tradition of Leigh Bowery, Boy George, or Bowie,
dresses to astonish and subvert. Blue lipstick, beard
stubble, fab shoes, frocks, mad hair, attitude. What
Travis isn't, however, is a woman.

I have to stop reading. I had thought that surely, after all
this time, it would be good to hear what the other side is
saying. What if it wasn't as bad as I thought it was? Yet, as if
the writer's commenting so acutely on my physical appearance brings an excruciating awareness of how my body is
feeling in that moment, I am forced to close the laptop again.
My hands are shaking. I do not want to read it. I will not
read "Children sacrificed to appease trans lobby" anymore.
Instead, I print out the article and grab some scissors as the
printer clunks along. I cut out the title, as if staring it in the
face may help it be less scary.

## "Children sacrificed to appease trans lobby."

The words still cut. I do not know why this phrase hurts
more than past punches, or shouts, or stares, but it does.
    This was not the first article written about trans people
in a major newspaper, nor will it be the last horrible article
written about me—part of the package of being trans and
in the public sphere in the UK from the year 2017 to today
means it is open season on me for the UK press. The highly
publicized 2018 Gender Recognition Act consultation came
with an increasing coverage of trans people leading up to its

publication. As public opinion was being sought about trans people and their relationship to public space, the Equality Act and our rights were being discussed by a newly emboldened Tory government. In swooped many fearmongering and highly scrutinizing conversations about trans people.[2] I am less interested in writing an analysis on this particular rise of transphobia—partly because I am writing from within it, partly because many others have written on it far more extensively—yet also because throughout all of 2017, that was what I wrote about.[3] I consistently used the moment to highlight what was happening to trans people in the country, almost as a way to dissociate from the fact that it was happening to me. I wrote think-pieces, became the stoic and strong Black trans person in the face of a media onslaught, and continued to use the moment of analysis as a way to "prove" to "them" that UK transphobia was real and apparent. I know now, going through the experience of writing this book, that performing this analysis of context instead of analysis of self has stunted the way I can think and relate to myself and my body. I have learned painfully that I was not just robbed of my internet security that day in 2017; I would feel the ramifications of such a public shaming in far more intimate ways years later.

If you spend all of your time trying to prove to *them* that what is happening is real, what you are left with is no reality of how *you* feel. I am less interested in outlining the horrors of what has happened in our country, and more inclined to try to map out where the horrors have impacted us. With

2. "The Gender Recognition Act Is Controversial—Can a Path to Common Ground Be Found?" *The Guardian*, May 10, 2018.
3. I recommend Shon Faye's *The Transgender Issue: An Argument for Justice* (London: Allen Lane, 2021).

one Google search, you can read about all the ways in which transphobia in the UK has increased to alarming levels since 2017, and how this has been emboldened by dangerous media coverage, yet if we take all of that as a given—how does it affect us as trans people personally, rather than in the abstract? Beyond a think-piece trying to convince others of our pain, what are we left of ourselves to sit with? In conversations about safety, public space, and sacrifice, how does the trans scapegoat feel after all these years of withstanding the scapegoating? As I try to decide what changes I want to make to my body, or how I feel about my gender and its existing beyond binaries of man and woman, how can I be sure that nearly five years of targeted, relentless, and false media reports about both me personally and us communally have not seeped into my decisions about how I would like to be?

## "Children sacrificed to appease trans lobby."

I stare at the title now cut out on my desk.

I consider the word "sacrifice" in the title of the article, and think about who, in that moment, was sacrificing something. I think about sacrifice. I think about how in that week, I could not find the reviews online that called me "mesmerizing" or "spellbinding" because they were buried under pages and pages of articles picking apart my appearance. I could not go on Twitter and read the tweets from theater critics, friends, and idols of mine saying that my performance in *Jubilee* was a "revelation" or a "triumph," because to do so I would have to trudge through countless tweets threatening my life, calling me a pedophile, or sharing photos they had found online and enlarging the bulge in my dress. It felt like a sacrifice of the version of myself from just weeks before, the me who had walked into the theater starry-eyed about my dream becoming reality. A sacrifice of a moment I will never get back.

I read a tweet from a Black trans person who came to see the show:

"To see another Black gender-nonconforming person on a stage this big, it means something, wish I got to meet them."

I think about how, for the first week of the show opening, I had to leave through the private exit around the back of the theater, terrified that those tweeting that they would protest against the show would turn up. When I look back at the just-turning-twenty-one-year-old I was at that time, the version of me who had dreamed in their housing project that they would one day be on stage, I understand that so much of the realization of that dream was stolen from me due to the press attacks. And those press attacks only existed due to transphobia. The word "sacrificed" in the article headline feels like salt rubbed into the wounds, as it is clear that what is really sacrificed in the "culture war" against us is trans people's possibility, in exchange for safety.

On reflection, it feels like a sacrifice that trans people know very well—one I have spoken about in these pages—choosing between our safety and our joy. The sacrifice we make when filling out forms, choosing which option may fit us best rather than the thing we actually are. Or the sacrifice we make going to bathrooms, trying to guess how the other customers will see us so we can make the safe choice. Even the sacrifice we make when not correcting someone on our pronouns, choosing instead not to disrupt the conversation. I think of some of the people I have met who say, "My pronouns are she/they," and when you ask which they prefer, they say, "Always 'they,' I actually only want 'they,' I just want to be less difficult." All of these are sometimes characterized as "snowflake" problems, yet I keep thinking about the culmination of these sacrifices and their impact on our overall quality of life. Each sacrifice eventually mounts to a pile of experiences where we cannot not allow our full selves to be seen, setting up those of us who are nonbinary and gender nonconforming with an impossible task of learning how to survive.

I have been guilty of minimizing those sacrifices myself. As a waiter calls me "sir" and my body tenses up, or as I succumb to ease in the face of another doctor and look at my frame and say: "Yeah, I guess male." The infamous "Kim, there's people that are dying" meme pops into my head as I think about what it would mean to complain about what seem like such small moments. I think of the other hardships in my life—growing up with food scarcity, surviving dangerous attacks—and I minimize these sacrifices as not being big enough to protest about. Yet when I see the word "sacrificed" used in an antagonistic way against myself and my community, it is as if the bridge finally collapses under the weight of an accumulation of sacrifices, and the implications they have for all of our lives. Nothing is minuscule when it happens over and over and over again. Living in the accepted reality of both the gender binary and the transphobia that inherently follows, we lose our ability to imagine what it would be like to live in a world that didn't demand that we sacrifice the expression of our whole selves. In fact, not just those who are trans but everyone around us has simply accepted that to be alive at a time within the gender binary and its enforcement is to accept sacrifice. Gendered violence becomes a wildfire, far-reaching and uncontrollable, and we are too busy putting out the flames to think about what is being destroyed in the process. Too preoccupied with trying to get from A to B to wonder what it is we lose in the fight or transition.

The gender binary forces us to lose our imaginations, and we sacrifice a more complex and rich possibility in return for complying with it. We get told by someone else when we are younger that we are boy or girl, and then we are expected to adhere to what it means to be a man or a woman. Sure, in our current era, these definitions are changing and in flux, yet the world still essentially demands that we be one of those things. Not a mixture, not neither; we must pick and be convinced in our path of womanhood or manhood. To deviate, or obscure, or complicate is to be met with punishment—and so we learn from our early years that we must sacrifice some of our instincts for ourselves in order to survive. Which is why, when Janice Turner damned me those years ago, saying that others are sacrificed for *us*, the irony would have felt laughable if it had not had such terrifying consequences.

I stare at the cutout of the newspaper title in front of me. I grab a pen, with the aim of rearranging and crossing things out in the title. A task to make me refuse the temptation to zoom out, to bring myself into the reality of what it means.


"Children sacrificed to appease trans lobby."

I cut out the word "Children" and I replace it with the words "All of us."

I then swiftly cross out the words "trans lobby" and

scribble over it "the gender binary." The headline now reads: "All of us sacrificed to appease the gender binary." It feels more accurate.

I think back to the man in the club who spent years deciding whether to paint his nails, wondering if his partner would leave him if he did. The sacrifice he made of his self-expression for the need to stay within the parameters of what he had been told was acceptable. As a couple, they sacrificed conversations around their hopes, dreams, television, travel, love, sex to have multiple conversations around the fear of painting his nails for nights on end. I am sure I am exaggerating, but as his partner blurted to me how they had "the same convo over and over again" and I sensed some lack of comfort in her eyes, I drew an image of two people stuck in a tower, outside of which all the conversations and experiences they could be having were happening. Yet they were stuck inside, for months and years on end, sacrificing those possible lives for one where they debated what Steve would lose if he reached for the nail polish. Choosing the gender binary and its rigidity over and over again, instead of freedom.

## "All of us sacrificed to appease the gender binary."

The male and female signs on the changing rooms about which the article was written are no longer just the ones in that Topshop in Manchester—they are also the changing rooms in my comprehensive secondary school in 2009. This time, the sacrifice came in the form of a boy in my gym class who pulled me aside after a grueling game of rugby, in the era before I had the bravery and logic to skip gym. This boy had never really spoken to me much in school, and after that moment he never really spoke to me again, yet he would always look at my gestures, at my eyes, at the way I walked, in a way that at the time I was not so accustomed to, yet now I would recognize as the specific and frequent way that men lurk and obsess over the gender nonconforming, in the liminal space between disgust and fascination. I would often catch him staring when he thought I wasn't looking. I assumed it was just because he didn't like me—being a feminine "boy" at school can cause people not to like you—yet when he pulled me aside after this gym class, my assumption was derailed.

"You're doing that drama play right. Playing a witch?"

I braced myself. I thought, *It's just one-on-one, I can take him if I need to.*

"Yeah, and what about it?" That attitude from me sprung from the thousand protective walls built around me.

"I wish I had the balls to do it," he said, in a muffled manner.

I paused. Struck by how wrong my prediction could be. "I'm sure you could," I said back to him as he shuffled away, the resulting silence full of a possibility both of us were too afraid to step into.

We both knew that was not an option. It would involve too much sacrifice on his part. He would have to sacrifice his place on the sports teams and give up being scared of insults hurled in changing rooms, likely even give up his friendships with the other boys. Or possibly there would be too much sacrifice on the other end: for him to be allowed to play the witch, on stage in his glory, the community around him would have to give up caring so much about gender and its expectations in order to let him do it without abuse. They would have to pause and wonder what his insistence on choosing desire and joy over gender meant for their own actions and behaviors—and what, in turn, they were sacrificing too. Of course, gender's suffocating weight works precisely because we do not try and lift it; rather we let it topple over us and at least keep us warm in its crushing embrace.

Thinking of this story, of my childhood, of the many children around me, I realize Janice Turner's article is so insulting because children are already being sacrificed to the gender binary every day.

## "Children sacrificed to appease trans lobby."

I could amend the heading so it becomes: "Children sacrificed to appease the gender binary." I think not just of the presumed straight boy in the changing room but more pressingly of the trans kids I have spoken to over the years. How they must sacrifice their paths to knowing themselves for the comfort of those around them. Where, depending on who they are surrounded by, it might be a caregiver or guardian who places their insecurities and fears onto the kids, cutting off their ability to be themselves. I am writing this while the waiting time for trans people to access gender-affirming healthcare in the UK is increasing across the board, when states across the United States are removing trans children's access to healthcare, and other states are passing laws to ban trans youth from partaking in sports as their identified gender.[4] I think of a friend of mine with a trans

4. "Trans People Waiting Years for Gender Healthcare as Demand Surges," *Reuters*, December 7, 2021; "Arkansas Becomes First State to Outlaw Gender-Affirming Treatment for Trans Youth," *CNN*, April 6, 2021; "Mapping the Anti-Trans Laws Sweeping America," *The Guardian*, June 14, 2021.

child who tells me that the school will not grant her a key for a gender-neutral toilet, so the child holds her bladder all day until she gets home. She is eleven years old. I wonder what childhood freedoms are being sacrificed to uphold binary sex and gender? What joy and possibility could kids find on the athletic fields that are instead being sacrificed for the comfort of those upholding a failing system?

I am reluctant to use the term *gaslighting*, for in the year of 2021 it is another word the internet has run off with and twisted its meaning into something different than it had been. But as I look at the title of the article again, it feels like the reader is being intentionally gaslit into believing that trans people are causing harm to children—which is in keeping with how trans people are treated throughout UK media and society.

I take another look at the article. I move my hands over the word "sacrifice." I look at the opening line. I think of the optics of a white woman calling a racialized person's hair "mad," or saying I have "attitude," and I realize that none of these comments about my appearance and gender can be separated from my race. The writer will deny I am experiencing misogyny yet in the same sentence use textbook examples that throughout history have been used against those who experience misogynoir. I think of all the times my mum has mentioned people calling her hair "mad," or how frequently Black women are told they have an "attitude," and I see the same tactics employed against me and my body—whether they call me a woman or not.

I move my hands over the opening paragraph, and I land on the statement: "What Travis isn't, however, is a woman."

"At least she got one thing right," I say out loud.

I am definitely not a woman. This feels like the crux of

what is upsetting them. The anger is not only that I am not a woman in their eyes but also that I am agreeing that I am not one. I wonder if inside these words is a bitterness at how I, a nonbinary racialized kid, who the writer compares to the white, gender-nonconforming Leigh Bowery, not only want to enter a changing room to get dressed safely—but I'm doing so while saying, "I need this space not because I am a woman, but precisely because I am not one: because I am neither."

I cannot help but believe it is the *neither* that specifically angers not just the writer but the media here. Not just my refusal to believe I am a man, like the world tells me I am, but more my refusal to be either. Even the suggestion in the article that I am dressing "to subvert" gets at the crux of this feeling for me, that it is the specifics of gender nonconformity that they are angry with and fearful of. Gender nonconformity cannot be seen as something people are doing to align with ourselves, or to be at peace— rather, it must always be seen as designed to impact others. It is not as if, were I viewed as at least "trying" to be a woman, or indeed if I looked "like a woman," that the transphobia would be eradicated, yet I do wonder how it would shift. Of course, a new set of sacrifices would arise, but I cannot help imagining which ones would disappear. Without such bold gender nonconformity, I do not think my existence would be seen as such an abject political statement. I am learning that gender nonconformity can never be neutral.

When I read the word "sacrifice" again in the title of Janice Turner's article about me, it becomes ever clearer that the word is intentional. It feels obvious to me that the hate targeted at trans people—but more specifically, at those who also are not male or female—is coming from a person's own anger at their sacrifices to gender. How someone else stating what they are not and choosing to have autonomy over a thing most people previously thought was fixed can trigger an anger and a hurt that they did not opt out sooner. How another person's choices can bring up those choices they sacrificed themselves.

So often, when transphobic press mocks trans identities, and specifically nonbinary identities, they use phrases such as, "What next, will you identify as a penguin?" or, "Not man or woman? Next you will be saying you are an alien." There have been times when I have calmly stated, "Oh, sorry, I'm not a man: I'm actually neither." Within seconds, someone has spouted a response like, "Can we now all decide to be cars?" or, "Next I'll be saying I'm a Black Rastafarian lesbian"—often trying to pick something seemingly farfetched, or far away from their reality.

I think what strikes me the most, and why I believe there is so clear a link to sacrifice, is that in many of these examples, deciding they are not the gender they were told they are seems as far from possible for these people as, say, changing species. My assertion that I am not actually a man or a woman, and that I am not going to identify within a constructed binary of gender over time, is, to them, equally plausible as their becoming a penguin. In some ways, I understand why. The gender binary and its limitations are so heavily programmed into us even before conception, with copious research done on and advice given about how to ensure parents have the desired sex for their unborn child. Once in utero, curiosity and speculation about the child's sex abound, and gender-reveal parties grow more and more extravagant. Birth announcements filled with "it's a boy" or "it's a girl," celebrating the gender before a baby is even born. Throughout our lives, there are so many ways in which gender is enforced on us. The system of gender and its binary options are all-encompassing. As much as we can try to avoid it, it feels impossible not to be part of its system. Even those parents I know who have tried to raise their child in a gender-neutral way regularly tell me about the struggles they face as they come across the enforcement of the binary: in education, television, literature, language, and even themselves.

With that in mind, I understand why hearing that someone is neither man nor woman could cause an incredulous reaction: laughter or disbelief that this thing that seemed inescapable is being defied. Of course, we know the laughter or disbelief can never just stay there—the laughter turns to mocking or the disbelief turns to anger—but I do also think that all of these emotions come from the root of sacrifice. It is easier to be angry, or to mock, or to not believe something than to sit with the sacrifices one has made to the very thing they are insulting another person's attempt to escape from. Like a knee-jerk reaction to something that has had them holding their breath for so long: they cannot believe escape is possible, so instead they choose to mock.

I think of the minuscule moments that represent sacrifice to me. When I see a famous TV presenter compare my gender to becoming a penguin, I wonder what he might have lost to the same fight. I think of how a man once told me, drunk at a PR event, that he had never crossed his legs his whole life for fear of looking weak. How a dear friend told me that his dad had never told him he loved him because he did not want to seem like less of a man. How once, a woman in a smoking area started crying, saying she wished she could stop shaving but she was afraid of looking too masculine. I've witnessed enough moments like this to fill paragraphs, yet as soon as I write them down, they feel almost cliché.

Yet I believe that these are all examples of the sacrifices we make to the gender binary. We sacrifice a complexity that is within all of us in an attempt to adhere to a binary that we believe keeps us safe, or in power. When we read the examples, they almost seem false in their shallowness. We think, *Surely this must be a caricature of gender. No man or woman is really saying this.* The gender binary leaves us as caricatures of ourselves, composed of all the sacrifices we have made in order to succeed as "good" and "proper" women and men.

This means that when we see someone reject, disrupt, or deny the very thing we thought we had to buy into, we can feel cheated into disbelief. As if the biggest sacrifice to the gender binary is that of our imaginations. Gender in its current Western form has denied us the belief that anything could be more complex. I will never forget a man asking me on a night out, after far too many drinks, while I tried to avoid this very question: "Well, if you can look like that and say you are not a man or a woman, why can't I do that?" Without missing a beat, I said, "You can, go on." He stared at me blankly, as if choice over his body was too much of a foreign concept, as if the padlocks of gender were already far too tight for him to remove.

I am sorry that others are angry at the power of our choices. I have sacrificed too much for gender: I will be damned if I will let it take away my choice to say who I am.

I look at the printout in front of me. Littered all around it are the sacrifices I have made. The only word I can see is "sacrifice." The word "gender" almost looks like it has morphed into it as well: as if they are the same thing. I read the opening paragraph of the article again and think about how a grown adult is allowed to write newspaper articles about another person's body. I cannot stop thinking about my body: what it was then, and what it is now.

How nothing has really changed except my relationship to it.

What if the "mad hair" and clothes that "subvert" need to go, so that maybe I could go into a changing room and buy the dress without all of this happening?

I cannot help but wonder if even a transition, in the name of gender, feels like a sacrifice to me too.

For so many, the language around transition unlocks versions of themselves they could almost never imagine, providing joy amid adversity, an ecstasy in fulfilling who they are—and that is, of course, to be celebrated. It means that the fight for free and accessible trans healthcare must continue; I want my trans siblings to find joy. Yet in recognizing that we are not all the same, I cannot shake the fact that my feelings toward my own choices are different than that narrative. Within my own choices, my transition is clouded with the feeling of sacrifice: "If I change this about myself, maybe I will receive less violence," or "If I do this to my face, name, and body, maybe others will begin validate me and therefore I will have greater sense of ease." I know those feelings are not unique, yet in a world where we have to fight so hard for respect and dignity, it feels terrifying that my transition can feel like anything other than a decision motivated by personal alignment. Friends tell me I will feel different if I make a physical transition, that these thoughts are not as important as the feeling one gets from physical change, yet as I look at the title of Janice Turner's article again, all I can think about are the ways in which our realities are neatened for others' comfort. I definitely feel the story of my transness and my choices are evidence of the sacrifices we make for the gender binary; although I find joy within and around my transness, its setting is one of sacrifice. It is like making the best of an awful situation. In writing this, I'm wondering if anyone out there feels this too.

I look over the newspaper article one more time. The version I am editing now reads: "Everyone (but us more) is sacrificed to appease the gender binary," with Janice Turner's original writing still visible. I realize I am writing at a painfully early hour, because birds are making themselves heard in the way they only do at the crack of dawn. I say to myself that I am not a morning person, yet I remember that when I first moved to London, I would often wake up at this time and hear the birds then too. I would set my alarm for 5:00 a.m., and I would grab a dress and heels that I was too afraid to wear during the height of day, and I would go for a walk around my neighborhood. Even three hours later, the streets would be full, but in those early mornings, it would just be me, a few other dawn risers, and the birds. All staying in our own spaces, walking without dreaming of interacting with each other. I would not wear anything out of the ordinary—in fact I would specifically pick a dress you could buy off the most everyday rack available in a main street store—and I would walk through the streets. It did not matter if I had gone out the night before, or was about to have a long day, I would sacrifice sleep to be able to have this feeling of walking in the streets untouched.

I didn't tell anyone I did this; it was just a secret between myself and the birds awake at that hour, but it was one of the things I did in order to feel sane. In the same dress that could cause traffic to stop and drivers to shout abuse at me, or provoke burgers to be thrown at me or mothers to point with their children at me, I would glide across streets without any spectacular response at that time of day. Even the birds would not look at me. I would take the chance to walk without headphones—silence being another thing I sacrifice in order to feel comfortable walking during more populated hours. I let myself feel what it would be like to walk in a world that did not punish our seemingly small choices for ourselves with such monumental consequences. Some would say this felt like a sacrifice, forfeiting sleep for a sense of safety, yet I also found incomparable joy in these early morning walks—a freedom that was so addictive.

Maybe that mix of sacrifice and joy is something I need to think about with regard to my own choices for myself and my body right now. It is unrealistic to think that my ongoing transition will not contain sacrifice, a giving-up of something, or an acceptance of hurt somewhere else. Yet this does not preclude the notion that these choices could also bring me joy, or if I am lucky, an addictive feeling of freedom as well. I just wish so much of that sacrifice was not human-made. I know it is possible to imagine a world where transitioning can be done without sacrifice, and that is what feels hard to resolve.

I look at the word "sacrifice" again, written on the newspaper clipping, as I talk to my friend on the phone. They are a Black trans nonbinary person, if we are using language that fails us, and they are my best friend and a sister, if we are choosing words of more importance. I tell my friend the story of my setting my alarm for five in the morning so I could walk outside safely. They respond without even taking a moment to pause. In a quiet tone that sounds a bit like a surrender, they say, "Well, of course, it's all part of the contract."

I think about that, in silence, for a moment. I wonder what contract they mean, yet I feel I already know the answer: The contract of being trans, but somewhere in-between, not a legible gender, racialized, assigned something at birth that does not feel right, existing in a liminal space that is not quite defined.

"What is your part in the contract?" I ask, with the same casualness I'd ask someone if they want anything from the shop.

"Well, I've given up really saying I am trans. I can't be bothered."

I am not sure I was expecting that: yet also, when I hear it, I completely understand. This sacrifice comes from being too tired to continually correct people's assumptions about our bodies and instead choosing to reserve energy for other things. We unpack the statement a bit together: my friend talks about how it is more depressing to try and fight for inclusion in the word "trans" than just to leave that fight altogether. We share our nerves about taking up space where we feel we do not deserve it. They mention that it feels like their choices are either to change medically and be seen as a woman, or to quit and allow people to misgender them in exchange for the peace of not fighting. They talk about how it feels like there is just one option or the other, despite feeling and knowing they are between things. We talk about how it feels impossible to both be seen in a heightened way and not be seen at all in so many ways. The sacrifices we've made in declaring our transness, and the sacrifices we may have to make to continue in it. We say this all with the casualness of talking about what we might eat for dinner rolling off our tongues, yet with a new anxiety bubbling underneath, wondering if what we may say to each other is too messy for us both to hold. Or if the feeling permeating this phone call—that we must have everything so stoically figured out— will leak into our relationship and we'll begin to doubt and question each other, discard one another for daring to utter an un-fleshed-out thought.

Neither of us have the correct answers about any of this. We both take comfort in our anxieties at least not being unique to ourselves. Yet I think of all the people we will never fully know because they have sacrificed being themselves for ease. How gender nonconformity is erased due to our lack of ability to protect it.

I look at the word "sacrifice" again. It is impossible not to think of death.

o

I had to take a break from finishing this chapter as there was news in our community of a friend dying. They were trans and Brown, and, among many other things, they were neither male nor female. Some will say they killed themselves, yet I believe it was the state that killed them. It was waiting lists to see doctors that never seem to shorten, cuts to disability services, a world that creates isolation if you cannot access it in the same way as the rich or the cisgender. It is devastating that as I write this, it could be about many people I know. At my young age, I know of too many trans people who are no longer with us, some explicitly naming their gender and the state's response to it as the reason they are no longer here, others leaving clues in remembered phone conversations, or old Facebook statuses. I think of how this is a sacrifice of peace, which the gender binary does not deserve to take. I think of the audacity of the "debate" constructed between "us" and "them," or the "trans lobby" these articles mention. In this debate over our lives, there is only one group with disproportionately high rates of youth suicide. Among all the big and small ways people may change themselves for the gender binary, there is the ultimate change of no longer being alive.

I think of my lowest moments—after being attacked, or sometimes just after looking in the mirror—and I think about the energy it took me to continue. In that split second, deciding that I would try another day, yet knowing so well that my decision could easily have been different. And I know there must be so many others that chose the alternative path in that split second because the world has made it impossible for them to exist while figuring it all out. Upholding the gender binary is seen as more important than our lives.

I look at the headline I have now crossed out and edited. The words "sacrifice" and "gender" bold and clear. The scribbled names of people who should still be here. I leave a space for the names I am yet to know.

I look at my headline, the one I reclaimed from horrors of the previous work. It still reads: "All of us sacrificed to appease the gender binary." And I think of how inescapable that truth is.

# 7

# "This is for us, baby, not for them."

Ever since writing the word "sacrifice" in the last chapter, it is all I can think about. It has made me want to rewrite this book and make that the starting point, yet reading it back, I realize that is what this book is: a record of sacrifice, an archive and memorial to what is lost in a world that cannot embrace gender nonconformity.

I am tired. The kind of tired I wake up still feeling. It is a tired that sits in the background of my days, a melodic hum just reminding me that this dysphoria, this gender, this thing I need to sort out, will keep eating me up if I do not make a move soon. I'm tired of not knowing how I feel in my body, tired of seeing debates around me, tired of not knowing if I am wasting my time trying to figure this out. It is all I can think about, to the point where I imagine others must be thinking about it too, even if we are in fact just talking about the weather. My mornings are becoming punctuated by moments of having to hold back tears. I am trying to be kind to myself, but it is hard when my own reflection in the mirror is the site of my pain.

In tears, I call my friend.

"I am not sure what to do. I can't tell my up from my down. I have hormones going to waste under my bed. I am losing my confidence by the day. I cannot tell who this is for—"

I go to carry on, but luckily, this is the kind of friend who will not let a hole be dug in front of her. "One: hormones are too precious to waste. So, if you ain't gonna use them, you know my address." We both laugh. Hers from the belly and mine from the throat.

"And two: I don't know if it's all this time inside? Or all this time online? But this ain't the bitch I know. What the fuck is going on?" she asks, with more calmness in her voice than I can portray on a page. The swears and the question marks make it seem like this was said urgently, yet the conversation had the pace of two girls talking about lunch plans, as if we had been here before.

"I'm not sure. I know I don't want to die unhappy with the way I feel, but I just wish I could stick this out. I am not a woman, but when I dream of looking like one, it's just so the dream is easier to talk about."

"Girl, I'm a woman because it is easier to say and I haven't got the time for anything else. Your mum is a woman because she was told she is one and it feels all right. Fuck, maybe she isn't, have you asked her? I never heard you so hung up on what everyone else thinks of you. What do you want to do?"

"I am not sure," I reply, annoyed at the fact that writing this book has brought me face to face with so many unanswered questions.

"Well, that is what you gotta figure out. It ain't about what they call you. They will still call you whatever they gonna call you, to your face, or behind your back. It's about what you want to do."

I go to interrupt her, but she beats me to it. "This is for us, baby, not for them." I whisper back, "I am not sure I know how to do that anymore."

Our conversation continues for another three minutes,

or maybe even seven. I'm not too sure, because after she said that last sentence, I decided, completely enthralled by the phrase, that would be the last thing I heard in the phone call.

As soon as the phone call ends, I go to my window; I need to breathe.

"This is for us, baby, not for them."

I say it out loud, to try to believe the words I know to be true. To feel them in my heart rather than just my head. I go to shout it out my window, in a corny act of reclamation that one might make on the precipice of either breaking down or breaking through.

"This is for us, baby, not for them."

Yet all that comes out is a whisper. I realize that I have been trying to speak in a more "feminine" voice on the phone all day. I cannot tell if I have been doing it on purpose for a while now, and I wonder when that was something I began trying to do. I drop to my regular register and I say the phrase again, in a raspy and deeper tone, allowing the words to fill me, unfiltered.

The word "baby" is what jumps out at me. As I repeat it again and again, it moves from being the term of endearment it was intended as and becomes a reminder to myself of my youth. Through its repetition, the word "baby" is rocking me, trying to remind me that it is okay if I do not know all the answers. That, like a baby, I could start again, and mold, and shift—learn to talk again if I must. The "baby" is reminding me I can change.

Despite most people's understanding of transness as being about changing genders, the ability to change our minds is not something that is often afforded trans people: we must be ruthlessly sure of our decisions about ourselves, no matter what age we may be. In working with countless trans people aged sixteen to twenty-five in the last five years, an observation I have made is that often the literacy with which they (and I, as I was still in that age bracket until the autumn of 2021) speak about their gender and transness is far beyond what their years would suggest. Or, more precisely, we speak with much more maturity and unshakable clarity on these subjects than on any others in our lives. It is not that young trans people are more "mature" across the board, but more that we show a heightened level of maturity when talking about our genders.

This makes sense: it is a byproduct of a cisnormative world, one that has told us who we were from birth and then given us daily reminders of that nonconsensual choice, forcing us to become extremely articulate in our denial of it. Waking up daily with the world telling you that you are a thing you are not, or trying to say what you are and being met with ridicule, creates the need to build a solid line of defense.

I imagine that if I were a kid who went to debate club, and we had the same debate topic every week over and over and over again, eventually my rebuttals would become robust, articulate, and sharp, simply due to sheer repetition. It is not that the argument I would be making would be untrue—one most definitely believes in it at first—yet to withstand the consistency of doubt I must embrace rigidity: I cannot show any doubt, because if I do, it will prove all those against me right. If there is not even a box for my gender on a form, let alone an understanding of it within most people I meet, then I must be a really strong person with firmly held convictions to hold this gender. I must build a rigid defense.

Yet as I hear "baby" echoing around me in my friend's voice, and I think how stuck I am not knowing what to do about my face and my body, I realize that gender and the culture around us have also robbed us—or at least, definitely me—of the opportunity to be unsure. I wonder how much time I have spent in a state of over-assertion, being unshakably clear in my lack of gender, having to fight for it at every single moment.

And I wonder whether what I am left with is an inability to be unsure of something, until I have no ability to explore, too afraid that if I show an ounce of doubt, or sliver of change, I will be punished. The perils of a transphobic country and binary gender system are that they suffocate any chance of exploration. Much of the anti-trans narrative holds that the promotion of transness pressures young gender-nonconforming kids to transition (as if that is a bad thing),[1] whereas I believe that—ironically—the cause is the limitations and restrictions placed on us by a transphobic state and failing medical system that take away our ability to spend more time exploring: we are *forced* to be sure at such a young age.

I cannot have any doubt. I know I am this because the world makes it impossible for me to be unsure. Likewise, because the medical system and healthcare surrounding trans people is so insufficient and gatekept, we do not have the freedom to approach this part of our lives with doubt. Even if we feel doubt, showing any sign of it feels punishable—like the "gotcha" moment they were waiting for. Even in writing the very first chapter of this book, admitting I may not have been born trans felt like admitting a dirty secret that proves the skeptics right: that I am false, and should be ejected back to manhood where I belong.

1. "Politicised Trans Groups Put Children at Risk, Says Expert," *The Guardian*, July 27, 2019.

I think of my friend telling me to ask my mother if she feels like a woman, and wonder if there was doubt there too, and if cisgender femininity allows for a space of doubt in a way that transness cannot. Or perhaps it is more that if you look "cis" (whatever that means), you are allowed to have more doubts and questions around your gender. Whereas, if you resemble the in-between, or the unconventional, you must be steadfast in that to combat any outside prejudice. The double standards on trans people to be so sure of ourselves, confident in our self-knowledge, limit our full humanity and honesty. Even in the external expression of my gender, I feel a pressure to prove my femininity in dresses and skirts for even the most casual of days in order to be read as "real," whereas my cisgender female friends enjoy the realities of not being a woman in the 1950s and are able to wear trousers.

When you are trans and feminine, your gender is constantly on trial—and in order to convince the jury of it, you must provide watertight evidence of yourself, even if that includes hiding some of the less tidy parts. I believe I am currently sitting with the effects of years of being on trial. Alone in my room, it is hard to figure out what I honestly want.

But my friend's words repeat in my head: "This is for us, baby, not them," screaming at the words I am typing: "Who are you trying to impress?"

I realize I have left so much up to *them*. Where *them* is other people's opinions, cisgender society, and not my own feelings. I've built an immovable wall around myself and my identity for protection from others' scrutiny. I've frozen my transition in time, because exploration feels like something

I could only do once, and now I must stay the same—or face eviction.

Yet I know this is no way to live. I know that transness, for me, has always been about honesty, and I will not let *them* rob me—us—of that. I try to think of what I would admit to myself, if it was just for me, and what I would say. So I go back to my window, and I whisper to myself:

*Right now, I am unsure.*

*I am unsure if I can survive happily in my current body. I am unsure if I can survive as visibly gender nonconforming as I am for the rest of my life and have the quality of life I wish for.*

*I am unsure what will actually change, both internally and externally, if I make certain alterations to my appearance.*

*I am unsure if it matters.*

I notice that the very thing I intended to leave behind, when saying I am nonbinary, is actually now a place I have found myself in. If you can excuse the convoluted way of saying this, my way of looking at my "nonbinary identity" has become, well, very binary. If I do this, then I must be this. If I do not do that, then I am not that. I've constructed a set of rules and parameters around my body, face, and gender presentation—that are ultimately wrapped up in how others perceive me. I am guilty of applying rules to something that actually works when lawless. As if any one gender is the same. I am guilty of deciding that if I want to be called "she" by a waiter, or if I enjoy a group of strangers mistaking me for a woman, then that must mean I am no longer nonbinary. Or because some days I do not want to wear dresses, but in fact I want to grow my beard out and try baggy clothing, that suddenly I must not be feminine. As soon as I write down these sentences, I know that this is antithetical to how

I used to see my gender. That eighteen-year-old bearded cross-dresser refused to be worn down by something as changeable as someone else's opinion. Ultimately, I have forgotten that the initial act of deciding I am not man or woman was to gain autonomy for myself, not to lose it.

I have fallen down a hole that has been dug by someone else, yet it feels like I do have the option to get out of it: I am just not sure if I have the energy. While my defiance of others' expectations used to feel like jumping from a cliff into water—scary at first, but so worth the thrill—now it feels like the most difficult swim upstream. I know it is possible, but exhaustion will be part of the journey. Would it be so bad to surrender and float downstream to them, even if it means losing a part of myself in the process?

## "This is for us, baby, not for them."

The words ring round my head. This time not as casually as when they were said to me on the phone by my friend, but more like the way a siren wakes you up in the middle of the night. Familiar yet frightening. I know I have said this phrase before, yet this time it feels scary because I do not know if I can find the truth in it. The "us" feels stuck together with the "them," and I am not sure where the "I" could be found within it.

Am I the me who was walking out with unshaven legs, beard on show, and wearing tight cocktail dresses? Is the me who was engulfed in this idea of doing gender solely for how I would feel just growing up now and becoming more realistic? Is that me realizing that eventually, the "us" I'm doing it for gets too tired, too under-resourced, too downtrodden to continue? And that the "them," when taken into consideration, given some thought, and appeased at least slightly, may offer comfort?

I know there are exceptions to the rules. I know this could also just be my younger age showing, that there are queer elders who will come in and say, "Baby, we have survived, we have done it, we have always been here." I know there are history books that show how gender nonconformity has existed differently, and arguably sometimes less rigidly, in certain cultures precolonization, and that the gender binary is part of a project of control rather than something "natural."[2] I can know that is all true, yet it does not change how I feel. Two truths can exist side-by-side, like the truth that we have always been here, that gender nonconformity is as old as time, and that when I walk outside I can go days without seeing another person who looks like me but only hours without witnessing another example of how hard it is to do this. Loneliness is its own type of endurance.

I know when my friend said to me on the phone that "this is for us," she meant to tell me that I have to do what will bring me back home to myself, what aligns me with the most happiness. Yet all these words are said as if they are not connected to each other. As if happiness is neutral and not tainted by what is around us. As if safety does not sit next to happiness, or validation does not come close to it either. As if "choosing what makes me happy" is not related to the money I have in my bank account, or could not affect the money potentially coming in. As if we exist as singular islands, where our choices for ourselves and our bodies

---

2. This concept is discussed in Thomas Laqueur, *Making Sex: Body and Gender from the Greeks to Freud* (Cambridge, MA: Harvard University Press, 1992).

are made in isolation from those around us, where we can pretend that each choice is only affected by or affects only us. But that is not true. We know that people make choices for survival every day. We know that the *them* is constantly affecting the *us*.

It feels wrapped in an age-old debate around our bodies and choice, one that expands beyond trans people's relationships with our bodies and touches everyone's decisions about how to feel good about their bodies in a world with rigid and unattainable beauty ideals. In a world that rewards those who are seen as successful in their gender—meaning beautiful—and where beauty is wrapped up in size, shade, and gender conformity, I cannot pretend that the path or choice I may take for *me* is not also for the benefit of being seen as successful by *them*.

So many choices people make, from shaving, to plastic surgery, to teeth whitening, to dieting, are individual choices, yet they are of course influenced by the ways in which society dictates who is worthy and who is not. Even bringing it up here, I can imagine readers eye-rolling at how obvious this statement is, yet it feels strange for me to leave this out in a conversation around my body and its changes. Why do I have to pretend that my transness is separate from those similar pressures to conform to society's beauty standards?

I believe the effects of severe marginalization, cisgender gatekeeping of our medical help, and the continuous attempts to legislate us out of existence mean that we are constantly reducing the complexities of the truths in our transness in order to survive and obtain validity. But cisgender approval of how we enact our genders, and why we may do it, should not be a requirement for care, safety, and belief.

I wonder, if our transitions were not so contested or fought for, whether more of us would be able to speak publicly about the different combinations of motivations that often sit underneath our choices—and how those motivations can include not just discomfort in our own visible gender nonconformity but also a realization of everyone else's deep disdain toward it. If there was not contempt for us, we could be freer in our explanation. I have spent ten years wearing dresses in public, eight years doing so while being honest to the world that I am not man or woman. I have learned firsthand what the world feels like when you are seen as a "man in a dress," the symbol of so many people's deepest fears and disgust. Maybe I want to change my body and my face to experience what it means to be seen as beautiful and desired by more people, rather than for some grand gender alignment. Is that not okay?

It is not as though we are not all aware how addictive feeling desired can be, how it can also wield power. Like many people, I have spent periods of time overanalyzing my online self—counting likes and obsessively refreshing a page to see who has seen what post. One of my most shameful addictions I have yet to conquer is the internet. But it is through this obsession that I have the facts to prove that the more I have presented in line with a conforming femininity, and the more my gender becomes legible under even trans standards of conformity (which feels like an oxymoron in itself), the more I am praised. If I look at my most liked photos on Instagram, they are the ones where I have no visible stubble, a wig, my makeup done heavily to contour my face into more traditionally feminine features: those posts are rewarded with attention. I do not want to believe the narrative that people will reward me, or anyone, for conforming more to the gender binary, even within queer and trans communities, but when I post a photo on a day that, in the street, people were calling me "Ms." instead of "Sir," I see my comments flooded with people who have previously been silent. Suddenly, all the comments of "gorgeous" and "beautiful" feel tainted, as I wonder how conditional they are. I wonder if maybe I am seeing problems that are not there: is this just the paranoia that the internet breeds, suddenly blooming? But then I get four direct messages from different trans people saying, "Oh girl, you put in the work, you look good," and I do not think I am making it up. I know that "the work" here means doing femininity better, and "good" means conforming in a more traditional way.

This goes beyond online interactions. I've spent a few months this last year walking the street in far more gender-conforming femininity, working extensively to try and find ways to be assumed "she" over "he." I had never tried so hard. Before, trying to be "she" over "he" would never have crossed my mind. I'd take pride in being called "it" or asked, "What is that?" on the street. Yet the last few months I've been trying, pretending to myself that it was only to see if I could, rather than because I really wanted to know how it would feel.

My trying worked. It did not magically take away fear and harassment—being read as a woman in the street is dangerous, let alone as a trans woman—yet there was definitely a distinct shift in what people's reading of me felt like. More people smiled at me in the shops. Fewer people moved their kids away from me. I felt slightly more comfortable walking past a school. And beyond the good feeling this gave me, I noticed how this also translated to more material support.

As I was walking down the street, a man reminded me

of the harshness all types of femininity receive by calling me a "slut." Almost instantly, two women ran over to check if I was okay. Without a beat, the man was punished, as the women called him a "prick," asked if I needed to be walked home, and showed me profuse concern.

I thanked them sincerely and said I was fine, because I was. In fact—if I'm honest—I felt great. Shamefully, this was a moment of harassment that I'd enjoyed, as it felt like an acceptance into a club. Not womanhood, per se, as that is not a club I am interested in belonging to—more that this was a club where people can perceive you as a victim, not just as a perpetrator, of violence. I know that this shifts and sways along the contentious lines of femininity, yet as a gender-nonconforming person, I had rarely had a moment of being asked if I was okay after being attacked. I've had people film it, cheer it on, or laugh with their friends—but to be checked on by someone else in solidarity felt so foreign. Even being called a "slut" over a "pervert" felt different, like the danger was still present—as all of us affected by the patriarchy can attest—yet the venom was less.

It may have been the right people being in the right place to offer me protection in this case, and it is unquestionable that this "protection" is highly conditional: we know that for trans women, protection is stripped as soon as one is no longer "passing." I have to be clear: it is not at all safe to be a woman in this world, let alone a trans woman—yet I cannot shake the instinctive feeling that my more visible attempt to be passing as a binary gender also afforded me some protection, however small. Or, more accurately, it changed the way I experienced violence. The violence didn't disappear; rather, it morphed into something more recognizable, and therefore at least there were others who could see my pain.

Being called a "slut" over a "monster" bonded me to those women within patriarchal violence rather than victimizing me in a less recognizable way.

This all feels, if I'm honest, disgustingly sticky. I know that safety is not a mathematical equation to balance. Violence is not something to trade within. I know, deep down, that if I want to transition to "leave" violence, then I am setting myself up for disappointment, as violence will not leave but instead will only change. I also know that this "passing" experience I had was in direct relation to my proximity to other factors that affect gender—the lightness of my skin and my thinness, namely.

It feels sticky, as this is not how I want to view myself and my body. I do not want to relate my self to how they may harm me—I want to be able to live a life away from that.

But I cannot help being tempted: to be desired—even if this is dangerous—is more tempting than to be reviled. It is undeniable that to be more desired by society changes how positively one is treated, whether trans or not, yet when the idea of transness is highly personalized, it feels disorienting for me to sit in those choices.

I have an urge to make the choices and changes as long as everyone knows that I should not have to. That I should not have to shave to be seen as trans. That I should not have to tuck to be seen as feminine. That I should not have to change any parts of my body to be the gender I am. That all these things can be true while it is simultaneously true that life might not only be easier if I do such things but might also feel better. That transition can be a mode of survival.

I think where I am tripping myself up is that I do not just want a world where trans people of various experiences do something as basic as survive: I am committed to a world where we can be in our fullness. It does not mean I do not take the evidence of our survival as miraculous, unfairly impressive, tenacious, and resourceful—far from it. I see what it takes for us to survive in this world and I am in awe of the unique and specific ways each trans person survives. However, I think the reason I do not know how to think about my transition, or in fact what is next for me, is that I cannot think of anything worse than making a choice for a reason as depressing as my survival. I want to make choices based out of my joy, my pleasure, my freedom, and my intuition—not just to stay alive.

When I envision myself in the future, I see a version of me that is proudly and visibly gender nonconforming, walking to pick up my friends' children from school in a dress, my true self on show. I want and will this to be possible, because if I can imagine it, I am sure it can be. Yet I also cannot shake that I do not see it done often. So many of the gender-nonconforming people I have known disappear with age, and I wonder if I will too.

I think that is why I am so committed to writing this down, despite an ever-growing fear of what it means to put unfinished thoughts, possibly wrong sentences and opinions, on paper. I want to archive this version of myself as I sit in a liminal space. I need there to be something etched into the pages of this book that—regardless of where I may go next, in both the words I use to describe myself and how I may present—says I was once here.

I am increasingly frustrated that conversations that are messy, complicated, or beyond a binary of man and woman, or A to B, can only be held in whispers, behind academic paywalls, or drunkenly in bars with friends. I'm tired of the liminal space of gender nonconformity continually being seen only as something we pass through to get to something else, rather than a more complicated space that some of us have intentionally chosen to stay within. I'm tired of a departure from gender nonconformity being seen as something to celebrate, as if we were always destined to leave it. I do not want any changes I make in the future to mean this part of my life will be referred to as "just a phase," as if it's a light moment I have moved through. As if it is not one of the most intentional things I have done. Rather, this book can say that for me, personally, this was never intended to be a phase—until the gender binary enforced in the world made it impossible to be here.

### "This is for us, baby, not for them."

I repeat it to myself again. I try to think about what I want, not what *they* will think.

"This is for us, baby, not for them."

I wish the separation of "us" and "them" felt simple, that I could know where "I" end and "them" starts.

I think of that phrase again, the loudness of it increasing. I cannot conclude that these changes I want to make are for something as fickle as others' opinions. I know there must be something beyond that. I think about my friend who told me her transition was about alignment, and that I should look for where I feel aligned. So I sit still, and I close my eyes, and I repeat the phrase to myself three times:

*This is for us, baby, not for them.*
*This is for us, baby, not for them.*
*This is for us, baby, not for them.*

I caress my hands gently in my breaks from writing, trying

to feel what my body would want if no one was around to see it. I close my eyes to imagine it is only me, to see what is possible. Yet the vision is not clear, I cannot get to it, there are too many people in the way. When I do find myself, my face keeps changing, the hair growing and then disappearing around it, a bulge visible and then removed. I realize I may need to focus on something less fragile and temporary than my appearance, so instead I try to find my voice.

My voice is my own, and I can hear it speaking things I have said to others before. My voice has not changed in tone, and when it is isolated away from anyone else, I realize I quite like the way it sounds. It is quick when it is excited, raspier after speaking for longer, and sounds restless before a point has truly formed. I listen to my voice and think of some things I have said to others, rather than the pattern of hearing what is said to me, in hopes of finding the truth of *me* away from the pressure of *them*.

I hear my voice coming through, the sound of a train somewhere in the background. I sniff the air and realize it is thick in a way that England's never is, and I see my partner applying lotion to their shoulders. We are on holiday abroad and I have just met a family member of theirs. I remember feeling smug on the train: I knew I had won the family member over. I used quick-fire jokes and any lull in conversation to talk about *RuPaul's Drag Race*, which was a sure way to soften the reality of their relative dating a cross-dressing gender deviant. I knew my partner was nervous; I had been there before. It was a delicate tiptoe between wanting to hold space for my partner's nerves around their family's reaction to me, an understanding of the ways in which family tugs at our need for acceptance, while also having learned through experience to keep my own emotions protected—that I cannot hold others' shame. We had sat in silence for most of the train ride, verbally at least, yet regularly stroking each other's arms to speak in less audible ways. One stroke says, *This has been a lovely trip.* Another stroke says, *We did it, now we can be by ourselves.* A last stroke says, *I can't wait to get home to rip your clothes off.* Yet as I could sense the train ride nearing the last thirty minutes, I could not waste the idyllic setting on silence.

"You know we were trying to get your family to like me despite the fact that I am trans."

My partner jolts out of their daydreams. I feel slightly bad for bringing this kind of conversation into our journey. It was a tonal shift with no smooth transition.

"Like, let's be honest, it is about them liking everything else about me so much that they forget that they are viewing me as a man in a dress." I may sound like I'm looking for trouble, but I am just being honest. I guess those things are not mutually exclusive.

"I mean . . . yeah. On paper they would not like you, but in reality, I knew they would," my partner replies, desperately trying to return to looking at the mountains out the window. They're the kind of mountains that look like an old computer background, beautiful in their symmetry. I can sense that my partner does not want this conversation to continue. We have been on holiday, which includes a break from thinking about ourselves in this way.

"Right. But I think we've got it the wrong way round. I think they like me specifically *because* I am trans."

I get this look from my partner, one that kind of says, *I know I can't stop you going into this conversation, so get to the point.*

"My transness is the good thing, rather than a problem

to solve. Like, my transness is actually the gift." I pause after I say it, almost guilty of turning my partner into an audience at one of my shows, hoping they will give a round of applause for a speech that no one asked for.

Instead, they kiss me on the forehead and place my head onto their shoulder. As if to say, *I'm sure you are right, I know you are, but I think there is something else you would rather do right now, how about we rest?* And we let the next thirty minutes of the train ride return to another kind of conversation, the odd arm stroke and hand grasp speaking more than words.

"My transness is the gift," I say back to myself now. I know how true those words still feel. Despite the crossroads I feel at about what to do with my body and my identity, I still unquestionably believe in the gift it means to be trans. Transness has taught me so much about choice, love, and consent—that through reclaiming and retelling the ways we want to talk about our own bodies, we can open windows to other parts of our lives.

I think about what I mean when I say transness is a gift: it has brought so many friendships and so much creativity and community to my door. Transness makes it impossible not to be aware of how even the things that seem the most fixed can change, that if you are unhappy about something given to you without choice, there is a world in which you can change it. It is a gift to know that. In a world that is fueled by a capitalism that robs us of so much freedom, it does not feel obtuse to say that knowing there is choice within ourselves and our bodies is a gift.

When I think about transness being a gift, I instantly think of the best people I know in the world, and how it is not coincidental that they are trans as well—rather, it makes complete sense. For four years of my life, I lived in a house of Black trans people, and although I resist the urge to homogenize us, there were certain gifts of living together that felt distinct because of our shared experiences. Whether it was the way we existed in public together, turning walks to Tube stops into mainstage events, or our ability to bend the rules of language within our conversations about ourselves and each other, I know the depth found within our relationships was only made possible through our daring to be trans—and such daring feels like a gift in a world punctuated with shallow tendencies. Like a gift of knowledge or truth, not everyone can handle what it shows, not everyone is always ready for what it may mean—yet that does not stop it from being a gift.

When I think of transness as a gift, I cannot help but think in a spiritual way. Partly because of the religious connotations of the words "gift" and "knowledge," yet also because thinking this way helps ground me in something that is beyond the violence. I remind myself that in different times and places, gender nonconformity was not punished in the same way as it is here and now. In some times and places, living outside of gender binaries was seen by some as connecting with something higher—as a gift, almost. Remembering this confirms to me that this current moment can change. That it is not predetermined that my transness shall be persecuted. That there is a historical power in our gift, even if others are too afraid to stare directly at it.

I think about how absurd it would be to give a gift to someone every year on their birthday, only for them to smash it up in front of you every time you do. Each year, you spend hours perfecting their gift, pouring love and care into how it is formed, even writing a card explaining what it means to you and them—only for them to just smash it. Every single time. You would not go back to them. You would not put so much effort into ensuring they received another gift. You would, instead, find someone else who would receive your gift with open arms, who would give you something else back in exchange, and who would celebrate all it took for you to bring such a gift to the table.

I do not want to base my transness on cisgender people's definition of it. I do not want to define myself in relation only to them.

I do not want to play by their rules of what my gender should look like. If my transness is a gift, let it be protected by those who will cherish it.

## "This is for *us*, baby, not for *them*."

These words, said by my friend on the phone, seem to go hand-in-hand with the phrase "my transness is the gift," which I had said on the train a few years back. If I see my gender and its expression only as a problem, then I see it constantly in relation to *them*. If I see my body parts, face, hair, structure, or outfits as something to "fix" in order to make my interactions with *them* more pleasant, then although this bargaining makes sense in a transphobic and violent world, it completely ignores the me that positions the transness as a gift. It puts me instead in this tightrope-style contract with the cisgender dominant culture, where my relationship with them is tightly negotiated around what I can change in order to be accepted—rather than what parts of me they are lucky to witness.

Rather than base my transition on something as conditional as cisgender acceptance, or something as fluctuating as "passing" as "man" or "woman"—as if those categories do not constantly shift for many different people—what would it mean to focus instead on doing it for *me*? Or for *us*? To see the choices I can make about my body as a chance to exercise the gift of self-determination and make my own rules for myself, as a way to be more present for *me* and those around me?

## "This is for us, baby, not for them."

I remember some of the conversation that followed after my friend said these words to me on the phone. At first I had zoned out, because the power of the phrase had brought me to a standstill, the way it can happen when someone says something you know to be true but you are not ready to hear it. Yet eventually, I tuned back in to my friend's voice.

By this point she was midway through her sermon. "Baby, it ain't for them! You gotta be able to wake up in forty years and be proud of what is looking back at you. Imagine yourself in the future, how you wanna be, what you wanna be, and make it happen."

A pause to honor the power of trans friendship: the most consistent survival technique I know is to call up a trans friend.

I used to not be able to imagine myself in the future. When people asked what I wanted to be when I grew up, I just imagined the then-tiny version of myself in a tiny costume of a fireman or some other job's uniform. When I grew older and the concept of the future became clearer, I realized I still found it hard to visualize. I could see others in it, imagine my mother growing older, or lovers at the time aging, yet when I pictured myself I still could not see anything. I'd often copy and paste whatever I looked like in that moment onto the idea of myself when I was fifty or sixty. So, if I was talking about having kids when I was forty, I would picture the current version of myself with children around me.

I remember one time I was in bed with a partner, one of the ones who asked me what I wanted to call my _____, and our hearts were beating in that tempo often found after sex: slow but charged, vulnerable yet playful. They asked me, "What do you want to look like when you are older? I think you will have Gillian Anderson energy." I reminded them I am Black, and that Gillian Anderson is sexy but very much white woman vibes. But then I paused. I realized I could not picture myself. I couldn't see a version of myself aging.

It has always bothered me, not being able to visualize what I may look like in the future. Knowing I so desperately want to be there but not knowing how I want to be physically. Hoping that by then we will have found a way to evaporate into genderless blobs of our energy, talking to each other without ever being perceived. Sometimes I make jokes to my friends, when we talk about the future. I say, "Oh well, by then I'll have my titties," and we all nod and smile, excited at my visions for myself. Yet I have been saying that joke for four years now, and I still feel exactly the same lack of excitement at the prospect of making that vision a reality. I could do it, sure, but it is not a vision that moves me.

Other times, I try to imagine myself forty years old, a beard around my face and a suit on. I've started working out loads and I've found a gay man who likes me for my fun and free personality but has stayed for the muscles and just-acceptable femininity. We are both campy gays who are proud faggots behind closed doors, and we met on Tinder, where you can't hear the femininity in my voice anyway. Any time a sprinkle of my gender expression comes through, all my partner has to do is look at my physique, and he is reminded that we are safe enough to settle down. He looks happy; I can't tell if I do. Because I cannot really see myself in the image. I cannot really imagine that version of me with my voice still speaking. I feel I would have to run away somewhere new, start fresh, cut off contact with anyone that knew me, so no one could say, "We know this is not you, we know you are not happy." But at least then I would have safety. Some security. A break from harassment. Yet I am not sure any of that matters if I also do not have my voice.

My favorite daydream of myself in the future is when I see myself as Pete Burns, walking to get a can of Coke from the shop. I do not mean that I look like a version of Pete Burns, I mean that I literally am him. Pete Burns, may he rest in perfect peace, was an androgynous icon to me, yet to many his face was confusing. Heavy amounts of plastic surgery, razor-sharp eyebrows, and a still-harsh deep accent. Often, he said, "I'm just Pete," when asked questions about himself, in addition to saying he was a man. Yet in my imagination, it is the "just Pete" that sticks, in a way that our imaginations sometimes try to make things simpler for our own benefit. In my version of him, he's walking to the shop just screaming, "I'm Pete!" to anyone who dares to challenge him.

I think it is the "just Pete" of him that makes me daydream of being him. The way in which, through surgeries, cosmetic procedures, and glam, he almost avoided the need to gender, instead forming another category within his body. The kind of image that makes saying "You look like an alien" the largest compliment possible. I find it an admirable daydream.

The perseverance, work, and strength it takes to have work done to your body is not lost on me—even more so now that I spend most hours of the day thinking about it. To land in a space where others do not know where to place you, in an intentional extreme, feels liberating. I daydream of having so much plastic surgery done to my face that none of my phones can recognize me. That all the laughs and heckles I received in the past when leaving the house would at least now make sense. It doesn't feel sad. Rather, I hear myself saying, "Before, you treated me like I was not human because I was gender nonconforming. Well, now look: I have spent all this money to look like I am not from this planet— laugh all you want, because maybe now I am in on the joke." Something about it feels intentional. I imagine Pete Burns walking to the shop to get a can of Coke, and there is something in the image that feels like he has taken back control.

I just wish I could see my face in that image, too. Or that I could stop imagining what I may look like in the future, and instead work to create it. To move out of this stagnant space that the gender binary and its violent consequences have left me in. To stop thinking and instead to feel. It might be a product of sitting inside for almost a year during the pandemic: when you are outside and living fully, you do not have this much time to pathologize yourself. Instead, you are too busy doing. You have no time to wonder how something may be viewed, because you are too busy fighting for your right to do it.

Well, maybe that is it. I need to remember the *doing* within my transness. In my opinion, I was only trans when the world and others started *doing* things in reaction to me. My transness was a choice I made so I could live more honestly, and like the movement and power that came along with it,

I now have the choice to *do* what I wish. I cannot control what others may read me as, nor can I control how others may treat me, but I do have control over what I do. And I can make the choices that will leave me feeling like I can find a version of myself within them, so that my face is not a pixelated vision of me in my imagination.

The way the world punishes gender nonconformity is one of our greatest losses. If the gender binary was not so painfully dictated to us and we allowed people to own their genders more freely, we would have so much more life. It is impossible to navigate this world as visibly gender nonconforming and not to carry scars, impossible for the weight of all the memories of things said and done to us not to stick to our skin. Impossible not to feel how our bodies have been given to gender violence and the fights we must undertake to claim them back. But when I think of my friend saying "This is for us," despite all the knowledge of how the world strips us of our agency, it reminds me that it will all be in vain if I also let *them* take my choice. If, in all of this, I allow them to strip me of my declaration of self.

I do not know what I will look like in ten years. Even if I decided now what I wanted to do with my body, I still would not know. Surgery and hormones are not magic wands; they are unpredictable and changeable.

What I do know is that I do not want to be led by fear, or by sacrifice, or by others' projections onto me. I want to be led by my desire, my choices, and my ability to carve my own rules. Powered by seeing so many others create destinations for their bodies that are not dictated by *them*, I want to remain committed to forming myself in the way I wish— no matter the consequences.

I will not know the answer, because to know an answer

about something as illogical as gender is an impossible task, but I do promise to do it for *us*, for *myself*, and not for *them*.

## "This is for us, baby, not for them."

*In my dream I am about to call the doctor, the one I spoke to last time.*

*I want to apologize for not turning up to our appointment, and explain I just had to figure out what I wanted.*

*I repeat to myself before I call him, "This is for us, not for them," and as I am about to repeat it for the fifth time, he finally answers.*

*We talk, and he asks me if I have always felt this distress, if I have always "known you are who you say you are?"*

*I tell him, "I still don't know, but I do not think that is unique to me. I am sure you do not know either."*

*In this dream, I can see my face, but it is constantly changing. The hair grows and then is shaved, the shape is round and then square, my jaw elongates and then shrinks. But it does not feel frightening. The change goes in and out the way a tide would, with warning and care, like you know it is about to happen.*

*The change feels as natural as the sea. Almost as if it is supposed to be there.*

# Acknowledgments

I think any piece of art is the center of a web, stretching out with all the different people and moments that made it possible. This book feels like the biggest web, one where I wish I could remember all the moments and people who made it possible, but I feel I would have to write a whole other book to fit everyone in. The truth is, you can't be someone like me and do something like this without so many people believing in you, championing you, pushing open doors for you so you can even get into the space to begin to think about writing a book. I will not attempt to write everyone's names, but I will say, if you read someone else's name and it makes you think about this other moment, that reminds you of this moment where you told me in a smoking area that I "could do this," then I also thought of you too. And I want to acknowledge you here.

I do, however, want to try to name some people, even if I know it is a task that will always leave someone out. Thanks to my literary agent, Philippa. Thank you for your patience, support, belief and . . . did I mention patience? I have so much respect for people who choose to support people based on feeling and instinct, not evidence, and in 2017 I definitely didn't have ANY evidence I would ever actually get my ass round to writing a book.

Thank you of course to my publisher, Canongate. Particularly, but not limited to, my editor Hannah Knowles. Maybe in describing Hannah, it can be as an emblem for the whole energy of Canongate and why I chose them to publish this book. Hannah has shown unwavering belief in me, without fear of what I may say, and rather excitement in polishing how I say it. Thank you, Hannah, for reminding me that risk is not something to avoid, but rather something we should run toward in art. I will never forget your support and work on this book. It is a support that has echoed through every part of Canongate.

Thank you to Gabrielle Chant for the final edits on this book. I've never had to do edits like this on anything in my life. You met my nerves, fatigue, and lack of experience with such care, skill, and a joint goal in believing in the need for this book. I learned a lot through our email exchanges and Word documents.

For this US version, I would like to thank the work of Feminist Press, particularly Margot Atwell, for the acquisition of my book. To cross the pond with this book is a great privilege, and one that could not have been done without Feminist Press's belief and kindness toward this work. It is an honor to sit alongside such incredible publications.

Thank you, Jackson, for being the first trans person to give me feedback on the whole manuscript. For your intelligent and sharp feedback to help me be the best I can be. I adore your work and your mind, and I cannot wait to read your work for years and years to come.

Thank you to the Crawford family: Mike, Zoe, and Karis. Thank you for being my home away from home, for treating me like your own, for letting me write the whole book in your lovely house and only asking about "how's it going?" when you could tell I wanted to speak about it. Your generosity, love, humor (and obvs food!!) made the whole experience possible. Thank you.

Thank you to Alok, my sister. For making me feel like I can do anything. For pushing me to be better than I think I can be. For changing my life. For always rooting for your girls to push harder. This book would not exist without you. I love you.

Thank you to Luke and Temi. Two friends who in different ways represent reminders of how deep a friendship can be. How friendship entangles our achievements with each other. You needed me to finish this book for us, not just for myself. You both hold me down in ways I am forever in awe of. I am so proud of us for doing this.

To my sisters, Danielle, Ebun, and Malik, no work exists without you three. Even if we can't sit down and read a book together. I thought about you all and what we taught each other through living together throughout this. Thanks for making trans a verb for me. And a fucking fun one at that.

There are definitely so many more people to thank. As I said, one person makes me think of another. I think of friends and I think of all my pals in my visibilityisatrap Instagram (RIP) who continually cheer me on, like Claire and Tom cheering from the WhatsApp messages that this is something I can do too. That cheer reminds me of artists and friends like Dean Atta, Scottee, Linda Stupart, and Rikki Beadle-Blair who have championed my work in the form of opening doors and lending ears. Lending ears makes me think of Meg, who in the early stages of this book told me how important finishing this would be. Importance makes me think of Kuchenga, whose own writing and devotion to her craft reminds me of the need to write Black trans books for the UK. Or Stacey ringing up her dad to get him to preorder the book reminds me of the ways it takes a village to raise anyone up, to finish anything, to celebrate at all.

So, to my village: I could not possibly write you all down. But I have tried.

I have thought about you. & I am so grateful.

PHOTO © GRIFF TOWNSEND

**TRAVIS ALABANZA** is an award-winning writer, performer, and theater maker. After being a recipient of the artist-in-residency program at Tate Galleries, Alabanza toured their debut show, *Burgerz*, internationally to sold-out performances in London, São Paulo, and Berlin, and won the Edinburgh Fringe Total Theatre Award. Their writing has appeared in *The Guardian*, VICE, *gal-dem*, and BBC Online, and they previously had a fortnightly column in *Metro*.